All-Color Guide

Cats

of the World

Matt Warner

A Ridge Press Book

Bantam Books
Toronto · New York

D0424491

Photo Credits

BC   Bruce Coleman

Creszentia and Ted Allen: 25 (btm.), 26, 27, 29 (top & btm.), 33, 41, 43 (top rt. & left), 44, 45, 46–47, 49 (top), 51, 53 (top), 55 (top & btm.), 57, 59 (top), 60, 61 (top & btm.), 62, 64, 65 (top), 66, 67, 68, 69 (top & btm.), 71, 72, 73 (btm. left & rt.), 74, 76, 77, 79 (top & btm.), 80, 81 (top), 83 (top & btm.), 84, 85, 86, 87, 88, 90, 91 (top), 92, 93 (top & btm.), 95 (top & btm.), 96, 97 (top & btm.), 98, 99, 100, 101, 102–103, 104 (top & btm.), 106, 107, 108 (top & btm.), 113, 116, 122, 123, 125 (top & btm.), 126, 136 (top & btm.), 137, 139, 144 (top, center, btm.), 145, 147 (left & rt.), 151, 155; Jen and Des Bartlett (BC): 12, 22; The Bettman Archive: 15; Lee Boltin/Metropolitan Museum of Art: 9; Brooklyn Museum, Charles Edwin Wilbour Fund: 11 (top left); Jane Burton (BC): 35, 50; J. H. Carmichael, Jr. (BC): 18 (btm. left); Bruce Coleman: 5 (top & btm.), 39, 141; Cooper-Hewitt Museum of Design: 13 (top); Culver Pictures, Inc.: 14 (btm.); E. R. Degginger: 17 (top & btm.), 18 (top), 21 (btm.); G. D. Dodge and D. R. Thompson (BC): 21 (top); New York Public Library: 14 (top); Pierpont Morgan Library: 14 (top); H. Reinhard (BC): 40, 78, 81 (btm.), 89, 91 (btm.), 94, 114, 121; L. Riley (BC): 129, 131 (left); Scala/Museo della Terme: 12; Scala/Prado: 13 (btm.); Albert Squillace: 7, 30 (all), 31, 37; Diana and Rick Sullivan (BC): 18 (btm. rt.); Sally Anne Thompson: 25 (top), 49 (btm.), 53 (btm.), 56, 59 (btm.), 63, 65 (btm.), 70, 73 (top), 75, 82, 110–111, 119 (top & btm.), 131 (rt.), 132, 134, 143.

Front Cover: Red Tabby Persian, H. Reinhard (BC)
Back Cover: Striped Tabby Shorthair, H. Reinhard (BC)
Title Page: Siamese, Jane Burton (BC)

CATS OF THE WORLD
A Bantam Book published by arrangement with The Ridge Press, Inc.
Designed and produced by The Ridge Press, Inc. All rights reserved.
Copyright 1976 in all countries of the International Copyright Union by
The Ridge Press, Inc. This book may not be reproduced in whole
or in part by mimeograph or any other means, without permission.
For information address: The Ridge Press, Inc.,
25 West 43rd Street, New York, N.Y. 10036.
Library of Congress Catalog Card Number: 76-9396
ISBN 0-553-13011-0
Published simultaneously in the United States and Canada.

Printed in Italy by Mondadori Editore, Verona.
098765432

Contents

6 A Common Cat Does Not Exist

8 The Origin of the Cat
10   Cats Through History
16   The Cat's Family

24 What Makes Your Cat Special
26   A Cat's Eyes
28   Claws
28   Ears
31   Teeth and Tongue
31   Whiskers
32   Sense of Smell
32   The Cat's Meow and Other Noises

34 Your First Cat

38 Breeds
42   Abyssinian
44   Balinese
46   Birman
48   Black Persian or Longhair

50   Black Shorthair
51   Blue-cream Persian or Longhair
52   Blue-cream Shorthair
52   Blue Persian or Longhair
54   Burmese
56   British Blue
57   Cameo Persian or Longhair
58   Chinchilla
60   Cream Persian or Longhair
60   Cream Shorthair
62   Egyptian Mau
63   Havana
64   Himalayan or Longhaired Colourpoint
66   Japanese Bobtail
67   Korat
68   Maine Coon Cat
70   Manx
72   Rex
74   Red Self
75   Russian Blue
76   Scottish Fold

77	Siamese	128	Belling the Cat
84	Smoke Persian or Longhair	130	Collars and Leashes
		131	Climbing into Trouble
86	Sphinx (Hairless) Cat	133	Tricks
87	Tabby Persian or Longhair	134	Grooming
		137	Bathing
90	Tabby Shorthair	138	Traveling
94	Tortoiseshell Persian or Longhair	141	Getting Old
96	Tortoiseshell Shorthair	**142**	**Your Cat's Good Health**
98	White Shorthair	
99	White Persian or Longhair	143	First Aid for Cats
		145	When to See the Doctor
102	**Show Time**	146	Common External Ailments
110	**From Mating to Motherhood**	147	Worms
		149	Skin Diseases
112	So You Want More Cats	150	Accidents
115	You Play Midwife	152	Internal Ailments
117	Newborn Kittens	154	Giving Your Cat its Medicine
118	**Room and Board**		
121	Feeding Kittens	156	Cat Organizations
124	A Place to Sleep	157	Bibliography
126	Good Habits	158	Index

A Common Cat Does Not Exist

Of all the animals with which man has cohabited, the cat remains most mysterious. As a pet the cat depends on people for its well-being and comfort, yet it refuses to submit wholly, as dogs do, and to this day, after nearly 5,000 years of association, it still is socially and psychologically independent of mankind. No one who has a pet cat can ever claim total domination of his charge. He gives when the cat asks, but when he asks the cat to give, the cat complies only when it is confident that a reward is forthcoming.

Why do people tolerate what seems to be such a haughty, insolent, selfish, and demanding pet? Because they soon learn that these are projections of human traits onto the feline personality and that the real nature of the cat has much to offer human friends. Cats do get their way, but they do not ask often. Most of the time a cat is a quiet, unobtrusive companion, giving you the same respect that it expects in return. Ordinarily it asks only when it cannot get what it wants itself or when you have conditioned it to expect a particular service. Then it can be incessantly demanding. But a cat is amazingly clever. Left to its own devices it can do surprising things, such as opening doors, drawers, and boxes, sometimes for no better reason than to satisfy its insatiable curiosity.

Few creatures of the animal kingdom are as graceful as a cat. It is supple but powerful, delicately beautiful but boldly brave enough to do battle with animals twice its size. A cat is candid

yet surrounded with mysticism. No other animal can make us so envious of its ability to relax and to exhibit such total patience. Not least important, a cat is clean and odorless, fastidious in its habits. A cat offers much to its people, and in fact, seems to have more to teach than it needs to learn.

Intelligent? Surely there is no easier way to stir an argument than to discuss the comparative intelligence of a cat and a dog. In many respects this is a futile exercise. Dogs are social animals, which explains at least in part their submissiveness. Cats, in contrast, are essentially loners. Their refusal to become puppets should not be interpreted as a lack of intelligence. Some **7** people might, in fact, argue that this only confirms their intelligence. If intelligence is defined as the ability to learn and to utilize previous experiences by remembering, it must then be acknowledged that the cat is indeed one of the more intelligent animals.

Your home is your cat's den—literally. Love of home and hearth is one of the cat's attributes. As long as you provide food and do not get new furniture or rearrange the old too often, your cat will be a happy and lifelong companion. It is independent, yes, going out if its way to maintain its *self* status. But it is also appreciative and affectionate. It has poise and dignity. In fact, there is little one could want of an animal pet that a cat does not offer superlatively.

The Origin of the Cat

Historians generally agree that the cat's association with man began in Egypt about 5,000 years ago, when small cats came in from the wild to feed on rats and mice at civilization's granaries. The cats were well fed and the Egyptians were appreciative—so much so that they coaxed the cats into continuing the relationship. Only a few generations from kittenhood to adult were sufficient to soften the wildness in the cats, and why not? Their new status had its advantages, too. This is the widely accepted explanation of the cat's domestication, but no one can ever be certain, for this was one of the humble facts of history, little noted at the time of its occurrence. It also is a relatively recent fact. The dog was a hunting aide and hearthside companion for **8** some 45,000 years before the cat ventured into human society.

▲ Egyptian cat goddess, Bastet

Cats through History

Subsequent steps in the cat's chronology are better documented. By 1500 B.C. Egyptian cats had become so favored that they were protected by law, raised to the rank of deity, and were memorialized in every form of art. Bastet, the female cat goddess, was believed to control the fertility of humans and their livestock. She determined the yield of crops, healed the sick, and guarded the souls of the dead. Owners catered to their cats' every whim. Anyone killing a cat, even by accident, was condemned to death. When a cat died its body was mummified along with similarly preserved rats and mice to feed it in the hereafter. Since mummification was a burial procedure only the rich could afford, it was proof of the high regard in which cats were held. (Centuries later more than 250,000 mummified cats were exhumed from one cemetery. They were pulverized and used as fertilizer.) Worship of the domestic cat continued for nearly 2,000 years, through all of the principal Egyptian dynasties. Never again would it command so exalted a position.

The Greeks became interested in cats to help control the rodents in *their* granaries, but Egyptian laws prohibited removal of any of the adored cats of Egypt and theft of a cat was punishable by death. Nonetheless, the daring deed was done and cats soon began to spread throughout the Mediterranean countries. At first, much of their distribution probably was accomplished by the Phoenicians—traders and sailors whose ships roamed the limits of the known world.

The Romans quickly adopted the cat and carried it with them on their missions of conquest. For some legions the cat became a symbol of cunning and bravery, and along the route of the **10** Imperial armies cats made themselves at home, the seed for

Egyptian bronze male cat ▲ Peruvian cat god, Chavin, as a motif in pottery. ▲

Roman mosaic of a cat and partridge. ▲

11

generations to come. Thus was the cat introduced into Great Britain. Romans treated cats royally, but did not revere them. They were engaging, utilitarian pets—nothing more.

By the Middle Ages the cat was in trouble with its former friends. Although barnyard cats continued to kill the rats whose fleas were spreading Black Death (bubonic plague) across Europe, this excellent service was not understood or recognized, and cats became the victims of shifting human values and, worse, of inhumane superstition. The now-flourishing Christian faith associated cats with paganism, and the belief grew that they were creatures of Satan and familiars of witches. Hysterical fear of witchcraft mounted until much of Europe was in its grip. Its supposed practitioners—often lonely or addled old women—were hunted down and destroyed, and so were their cats. Countless thousands of cats were crucified or burned, slowly and miserably, their howls of pain presumably venting the evil demons within them. Others were bagged, usually with some condemned wretch, and drowned. Still others were impaled on spears, shot through with arrows, or clubbed to death. Mankind was consumed by the notion that the extinction of cats would rid the world of whatever ills or misfortunes they represented. Some practical souls salvaged cat fur for trimming garments. Many cats—served as "rabbit stew"—also filled

12 hungry peasant bellies.

Illuminated Ms., *Four Cats and Two Mice* from *Lincoln Bestiary* ▲
Detail from *The Garden of Earthly Delights,* H. Bosch ▶

▲ Fifteenth-century woodcut, Germany

Aesop's fable—the cat and cock ▲ La Fontaine's fable—the cat and fox ▲

Cat killing persisted, fervently and relentlessly, though fortunately for the species there were kindly, less fanatic people that kept cats as pets and to help in ridding their habitations of rodents. Yet it was not until the 19th century that cats began to climb again into general favor in Europe and the western world. Vestiges of the cat's bad reputation persist today in superstitions linking cats with black magic and other forms of the occult, including such now-innocent expressions as Halloween. Only in very recent times has the cat's prestige climbed to a level sufficiently high to vie with the dog in popularity as a pet, but to this day people who dislike cats are vehement in their feelings. Through it all, the cat has persisted, a charming creature capable of capturing the imagination and warming the heart as it expresses itself in the natural processes of being cat.

◀ Detail from *First Stage of Cruelty*, W. Hogarth

The Cat's Family

All domestic cats belong to the same species, *Felis catus*, though there are more than two dozen breeds. Where the species originated is not clear, but small wild cats of northern Africa are considered to be direct-line ancestors.

The evolution of the cat family can be traced to a weasellike animal called a miacid that roamed the earth some 35 million years ago. It was this animal that gave rise to the dog family as well, and to many other carnivorous animals that we know today. The cat family followed the same developmental route as the civets and their relatives.

Two tribes of cats once existed, but one did not survive the Ice Ages. This tribe consisted of various species of saber-toothed cats, magnificent and powerful beasts with tremendous, ten-inch-long canine teeth. Despite the cats' large size, making them seemingly formidable, they were apparently slow moving compared to some of their cat cousins and other carnivorous animals with which they shared the world. It has been suggested that they were mainly carrion eaters. In the fierce competition for survival, at any rate, they were not the winners. When the curtain of the Ice Ages lifted, the saber-toothed cats were gone. No one knows precisely why they were incapable of bridging this period in earth's history.

The surviving tribe consisted of cats identical to those alive today. These wild cousins of the domestic cat number about 35 species. Like many other animals, the world's wild cats are rapidly diminishing in numbers as their living space is preempted by man. Half the feral cat species are on endangered lists, the populations of some reduced to such low levels that it is doubtful they can recover even with protective laws. Among those

▲ Spotted Leopard ▼ Lioness and Cubs

▼ Ocelot ▲ Cheetah ▼ Caracal

18

courting doom are some of the best known of all wild animals. Of the lot, only the domestic cat remains truly abundant and secure.

Lions were long ago pushed back from Europe to a stronghold in Africa, where they are now making a last stand in sanctuaries set aside for them. If it were not for these large reservations, the king of beasts—some males weigh more than 500 pounds—might not exist today. Even so, the survival of the lion is precarious. In Asia, where it once roamed widely, it has been reduced to a few hundred that live in the Gir forest of Gujerat, in western India.

The tiger, about the same size as the lion, is less fortunate. Its status now is precarious, and the few remaining animals are still preyed on by man for trophies, for skins, and for exhibition. Admittedly, any cat as large as a lion or a tiger can be formidable, but places should be set aside where they will be safe.

The most unusual of the big cats is the cheetah. It can neither roar like other big cats nor purr like a small cat. Rather, the cheetah makes doglike barking noises. It also chirps, sounding almost like a bird. For short distances the cheetah is the swiftest of all land animals, accelerating to 40 miles per hour within two seconds and exceeding 70 miles per hour at top speed. It can **19**

▲ Serval

maintain this rate for no more than a few hundred yards, however. If it does not catch up with its prey and make its kill in a quick, short dash, the cheetah breaks off the chase and searches out another victim. Cheetahs were once tamed and trained by sportsmen to hunt and kill antelopes in the grasslands. Now the cheetah, the most canine of the cats and the only member of the family that cannot retract its claws into sheaths, is nearing extinction.

Jaguars, leopards, snow leopards, clouded leopards, pumas or cougars—all of the big cats demand extensive territories in which to hunt, and all have also been hunted by man for sport, for their hides, and to rid the land of "varmints." The few remaining animals can be preserved—the species saved from annihilation—only by the continued watchfulness of conservationists.

Many of the smaller cats are also endangered. The sleek and beautiful ocelots of the American tropics have been heavily hunted for their fur and also trapped for sale as pets. They are now listed as an endangered species, as is the margay that lives in the same region. Jaguarundis and pampas can both be added to the list, victims primarily of destroyed habitat. The lynx still survives in wilderness areas of the Northern Hemisphere, but its numbers are few. The closely related bobcat has so far managed to thrive even near human habitations. Two unusual and handsome medium-sized cats of Africa that are also becoming rare are the serval, a spotted cat noted for its swiftness, and the caracal, which has unusually long ears with tufted tips. The caracal ranges also into western Asia.

Asia also has its share of small- and medium-sized cats. Of these, one of the most attractive is the leopard cat, its intense

▲ Margay ▼ Leopard Cat

black spots in rows (rather than rosettes as in the leopard's coat) along its yellowish or grayish body. Its tail has a black tip and black bands. The ears are also black. At least half again larger than the common domestic cat, with which it has been reported to hybridize, this handsome cat lives in the forests and mountainous regions of southeastern Asia, particularly in India, and is found also on a number of off-shore islands. Hunting at night, the leopard cat accepts as fair game almost anything that moves—from mice to small deer and from birds of the forest to domestic fowl pilfered in villages.

The leopard cat's pelt is prized, and this is the greatest threat to the survival of the species. Because it apparently produces two litters a year with regularity and is also reasonably secretive in habits, keeping out of sight during the day in caves and inaccessible places, the population of the leopard cat has been reasonably stable and safe. Although there are exceptions, the leopard cat does not tame well and so has been spared heavy exploitation by the pet trade.

▲ Bobcat

Other Asiatic cats have not fared as well, or at least their current status is either not well known or is questioned. Among these cats are the rusty-spotted, an easily tamed but rare small cat of southern India and adjacent regions; the marbled, a small version of the clouded leopard living in the Himalayas and noted for its long, soft fur; the Bornean red, a wild and uncommon jungle dweller; Temminck's, a beautiful but little-known reddish gold cat of the heavily forested areas; Pallas's, with silvery long fur and an unusually broad head and low forehead; the flat-headed, a smaller cat that frequents waterways where it feeds on frogs and fish as well as on birds; and the Chinese desert, which inhabits the edge of the steppes but is so rare that not much is known about its habits.

Two cats, similar to each other, are considered to be possible ancestors of the domestic cat. One is the African wildcat, also called the kaffir cat. Ranging widely over northern Africa, it is about the same size as the domestic cat, with which it hybridizes freely. When angered, the African wildcat lifts a neck ruff as a threat. The slightly larger jungle cat was formerly fairly abundant in Egypt and other parts of northern Africa. The jungle cat is distinguished by its rather large tufted ears. Some authorities speculate that the domestic cat may have resulted from a mating of these two species many centuries ago.

We will never know, of course, nor does it really matter greatly now. What we have today is remote from either of these wildcats—or is it? It depends on the mood of your cat, whether it is day or night, and whether you cat is alone with its past or perched on your lap enjoying the pleasures of today. One thing certain: you cat will never reveal the secret, for being mysterious is part of its personality.

What Makes Your Cat Special

Your small cat, first cousin of the King of Beasts, is a well-developed bundle of muscles and sensory organs in a fur wrapping. Cats belong to the same order of mammals, the Carnivora, as dogs, bears, wolverines, and other flesh-eaters. They share with them such basic features as clawed toes, a well-furred body, and distinctive large canine teeth with which they hold their prey and then rip off flesh. Within this order, cats form a specific family, the Felidae, with features that separate them clearly from all other members of the order. Your cat is a classic member of its family.

Around the house your cat is most likely a calm, sleepy-eyed, purring creature. But how quickly that attitude can change! Bring a strange cat or dog into the room and instantly your cat's softness is converted to taut muscles. Its eyes blaze, and paws that have been as blunt as boxing gloves become lethal weapons, sharp claws unsheathed and ready to slash. The hair on its body stands out, the tail puffs, the back arches. It does not arch its back out of fear, but as an intimidating gesture. By raising its back, a cat appears larger than it actually is. And unlike the dog, your cat will probably stand its ground. Your once-docile cat is now prepared to do battle.

Or let your cat out into the night. A few steps from the door it becomes a silent hunter, moving stealthily on padded feet while its wide-open eyes scan the area in the dim light and its sensitive ears turn toward noises you cannot hear. In the night your cat becomes a beast of the wild, reverting to its hunter instinct. What are some of the characteristics that make the cat so distinctive, unlike any other warm-blooded animal?

▲ Outdoor pet ▼ Household pets

A Cat's Eyes

Large and round, a cat's eyes are set owllike on the front of its rounded head. They look straight forward. These are the eyes of a hunter, positioned for seeing every object of movement directly ahead. In contrast, the eyes of the hunted, such as a rabbit or deer, are at the sides of its head where they can see ahead, to the sides, and even to the rear in order to detect an attacker.

In basic structure, your cat's eyes are almost identical to yours. One difference is the "third eyelid," or nictitating membrane. Located under the eyelids, the nictitating membrane slides across the eyeball diagonally, giving the eye additional **26** protection.

▲ Almond-shaped eyes of a Siamese

Another difference is the tapetum lucidum, an extra layer of light-reflecting cells on the back of the retina of the cat's eye. This is what makes a cat's eyes change luster—chatoyance—and seem to shine when a light is turned on them. To the cat, this cell layer is quite functional, for it utilizes by recapture every available bit of light and thus aids the cat in "seeing in the dark." A cat cannot see in total darkness, of course, but it can see in very dim light. At night the pupils of the cat's eyes are opened fully to let in even small amounts of light, which falls on a retina equipped with a greater number of rods that contain visual purple (rhodopsin) sensitive to light than are found in your eyes. Eyes adapted for daylight vision have fewer of these rods. In glare, the pupils of the cat's eyes contract to slits admitting the smallest possible amount of light.

All kittens have blue eyes, but before the cat matures, different pigments may change the color of the iris. In some "odd-eyed" cats the two eyes may differ in color.

Though cats have superior vision they are color blind. They can detect differences in luminosity, however; so in effect they distinguish colors by differences in brightness. The cat's eyes are, in fact, sensitive to a wider range of luminosity than are a human's, but they do not see the differences as color. **27**

▲ "Odd-eyed" cat

Claws

Cats keep their claws encased in sheaths until needed. Little kittens play with their claws out. While they are tiny, the claws do no harm, but it is important for them to be taught early that their claws are not to be used when playing with you.

Cats use their claws to defend themselves and for climbing. It is controversial whether house cats should be declawed (see p. 135), but if a cat persists in being destructive or in scratching people there may be no alternative.

Ears

White cats with blue eyes are typically deaf, a genetic characteristic. But normal cats have exceptionally sensitive and acute hearing, to a level of 40,000 Hz. (far beyond the range of a stereo tweeter) or higher. Your cat, for example, is not at all disturbed when your car comes into the drive because it knows the sound of the motor. But if a different car arrives—even the same make—your cat is immediately alert, waking even from a nap to dart off to a hiding place. Watch your cat's ears twist both ways as they tune in on sounds beyond your hearing.

The base of the outer ear is cuplike, funneling sounds to the eardrum where the vibrations are recorded and transmitted by the inner-ear mechanism to the portion of the brain responsible for interpretation of sounds. Dust and other particles are kept out of the ear by a screen of fine hairs, but now and then a collection of wax and debris may become bothersome. The cat will dig at its ears to get relief, and in so doing may start an infection. To get rid of the matter, carefully clean the ears with a small ball of cotton soaked in mineral oil, but be sure not to probe deeply. A cat's sensitive and delicate ears should be treated gently.

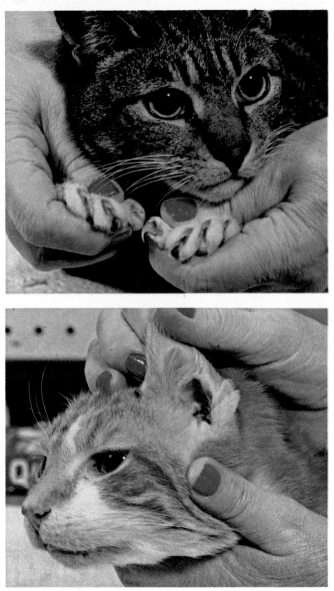

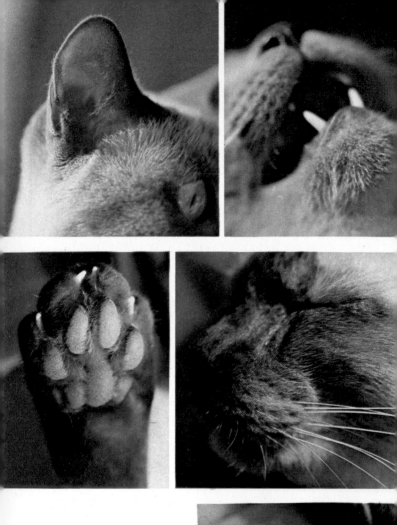

Teeth and Tongue

Adult cats have a total of 30 teeth—16 in the upper jaw, 14 in the lower. All are small except the pair of large, daggerlike canine teeth in each jaw, which help in holding onto prey. Because they are slanted inward slightly it is almost impossible for prey to get free. In addition, the jaw muscles are powerful. When a cat clamps tightly on an object, it is very difficult to get it to release its hold. Because a cat cannot chew, it swallows its food in chunks, depending on its strong digestive juices to break down the food tissues.

The cat's tongue is unique, serving both as a brush and as a rasp to remove the flesh from bones.

Whiskers

With its whiskers, or vibrissae, a cat can feel its way in the dark. The width of its cheek whiskers—that is, the distance they stick out at each side of the head—is equal to or slightly wider than the greatest width of the cat's body. A cat knows, therefore, that where its whiskers will pass its body can follow. The whiskers are effective organs of touch and should never be trimmed.

Cats appear slim-bodied and are able to pass through narrow openings because they have very small collarbones, which are not connected solidly to other elements of the skeleton as in other animals. This gives the cat greater flexibility and enables it to squeeze through tight places with ease. **31**

Sense of Smell

Cats have a well-developed sense of smell, despite the relatively small size of their noses. Inside the nasal cavity there is a large olfactory area that contains numerous tiny hairs. The cavity is kept moist by mucus in which particles must be dissolved before nerves can register them as a chemical stimulus and transmit·the sensations to the brain for interpretation.

In the wild, cats use their sense of smell in finding prey. They get great pleasure from particular odors, notably catnip, and some house cats even develop addictions to perfumes and powders. Cats apparently enjoy the odor of their food as much as its taste, and if their sense of smell is reduced or even destroyed by a bad cold or some related disease they may refuse to eat. Odors also play a significant role in a cat's sex life. Even at long distances a cat can distinguish male from female. They can also detect a neutered cat, which is rarely accepted by strange males or females.

The Cat's Meow and Other Noises

A cat can make itself heard like no other animal. The cat family, in fact, is commonly divided into two groups based on the sounds they make: the big cats, which can roar but not purr; and the smaller cats, which can purr but not roar. Both large and small cats make a lot of noises in between these two sounds to let their feelings be known. Your pet cat, as you know, is never at a loss for a way to express itself, and if you have a Siamese, it no doubt "talks" almost constantly. Even the ordinary meow is made with a great variety of inflections and meanings. Some of these you learn to recognize; others are conversation between cats. There is, for example, an angry meow that if not heeded may be followed by deep, throaty growls, hissing, and then screams. Most talked about, surely, is the caterwaul—the loud

wail of a cat at mating time. A caterwauling chorus is indeed demoniacal.

The sound of pleasure is the purr. How and why a cat purrs is still not completely understood. Many cats purr only in one tone, but some have different pitches and volumes of purring. When a cat is feeling comfortable and secure it may even purr very softly to itself while its eyes are closed and it appears to be asleep. The purr does not always mean pleasure, of course. You will discover that your cat has one kind of purr that is used only when it is frightened or when it is in pain.

No doubt about it, your cat does have its own language or means of communication. With a bit of study you can learn to understand it almost as well as another cat.

Your First Cat

If you already have a cat in the family, chances are slim that you selected it carefully. Most people are captivated by a bright-eyed, roly-poly bundle of fur with claws, and presto—a kitten has a home. Kittens can sell themselves even to people who never knew they wanted a cat. It may be that a neighbor offered you a surplus kitten that you couldn't resist. Or perhaps you have a soft heart for stray animals. If you do, you may be feeding several cats. The word spreads—among cats and among people. But once you do have a cat in the family it will stay. Cats have winning ways.

But if you do set out specifically to select a cat, how do you make a choice? If you decide you want a pedigreed cat, you must choose a breed (pp. 38-101). No matter which you choose you will be getting an aristocrat. Make certain you get the papers to prove it, because you pay a premium for a pedigree. You may not intend to put your cat in a show, but in case you change your mind you will have the necessary credentials. Still another possibility is that you may decide to sell your cat's services if he is a male, or allow a queen to have kittens. Either way, the pedigree can pay off handsomely.

Cats without pedigrees make equally good pets. If you let it be known in your neighborhood that you want a cat, you will probably get one for nothing. Or you can buy a kitten at a pet store for a small sum. You are gambling a bit on family history and personality, but you can also get a real winner in every respect.

Whichever your choice—pedigreed or not—start with a kitten, not a full-grown cat. You can enjoy its all-too-brief weeks of

▲ Tabby kitten

kittenhood and will have complete control of its training. Taking care of a kitten does require time, of course. If this is a problem, you may have to settle for an adult. Here there is one big advantage: You will know exactly what the cat looks like and can even be reasonably sure of its disposition. But most people do prefer starting with a kitten. They are then largely responsible for how it acts as an adult, and it can adapt to the family's ways while it is most tractable.

Select a kitten that is weaned, or about eight weeks old. If you are making your choice from a frolicsome litter, refrain from feeling sorry for the soulful, sad-eyed kitten in the corner. It may not be part of the group because it is ill or has a personality problem. Your best choice is the romping rascal that stays on top of the heap—or at least never stops trying to get there. This one is vigorous and in good health. You will be starting with a winner. And by the time it is eight weeks old, it will be ready to tackle the world.

But the kitten is all bravery and no experience. The trip from wherever you get it to your home is its first venture into the outside world, away from its mother and its brothers and sisters. This can be very frightening. You must do all you can to make the transition easy. Have its new bed ready, so it can settle down for a good rest. Kittens tire quickly. Let it sleep as long as it likes, and do not let other pets or small children bother it. When the kitten wakes up, give it some warm milk or a small serving of some suitable solid food. Then let it go exploring in its new surroundings. It will not take long for the kitten to learn its way around and to get the feeling of belonging.

Give other members of the family instructions about how to handle and care for the kitten. Children are sometimes uninten-

tionally abusive, playing too long and rough. Make rules and stick to them. Demonstrate how the kitten can be picked up or carried: one hand between the front legs holding the chest, the other cradling the seat and hind legs. The kit should be held firmly but without squeezing. Never carry it by grabbing the loose skin of its neck. Only mother cats can do this properly and without harming the kitten.

If the kitten is joining a household that already has an older cat or a dog among its members, it is invading private territory. With few exceptions, the resident pet's reaction will be a bristling rejection of the newcomer, or even an attack. Keep the pets separated at first. They will smell each other in various places around the house, and when it comes time for a meeting they will not be total strangers. Make the introduction brief and stay close by. If the usual pattern is followed, the kitten will soon be accepted. Fast friendships often develop, even between cats and dogs.

It will not take many days for a kitten to become a full-fledged member of the family, or many months to become a full-fledged cat. This makes it all the more important that you select wisely. You must get the kind of a cat that you will want to live with for the rest of its life. If you are a trúe lover of cats—that is, a felinophile or ailurophile—this will not matter greatly, of course. You love all cats, and because cats are wise creatures, the feeling is undoubtedly mutual. **37**

▲ Siamese

Breeds

Cats need no help in maintaining the species. They have managed this by themselves quite well for centuries. A cat in the mood for mating, whether male or female, rarely goes unsatisfied unless its owner keeps it confined—often no small feat in itself—until the urge is naturally abated. Given the slightest opportunity, a cat will somewhere find a cooperative companion and soon have a new generation in the making. As far as breed is concerned, the mating pair is not discriminating. A cat is a cat and more specifics are not necessary. The result is a tremendous population of cats with mixed ancestry.

Many cat owners are similarly unconcerned about the family histories of their cats. They even enjoy surprises in the litters produced by their queens and occasionally get handsome variations. But if they are interested in cats for show they get no champions. They contribute to dilution rather than to strengthening of the breed. The specific breeds of cats are maintained in purity only by careful selection of mates to preserve and develop particular qualities. Litters produced by controlled mating are examined closely, and those with weaknesses or undesirable features are not bred further; those with desirable characteristics are perpetuated. A breed is not established until, over successive generations, all kittens in a litter are predictably consistent in their characteristics.

The standards for each breed are established by the governing bodies of cat-fancier societies or clubs. These are the organizations that either conduct or sanction shows or exhibits in which the cats of various breeds are judged. Some associations deal **38** only with cats of a particular breed; others include all breeds.

39

▲ Chinchilla

Smaller clubs are generally affiliated with a larger organization so that rules and regulations are coordinated. In the United States, for example, the Cat Fanciers' Association, Inc. is a national organization with the number of associated clubs approaching 500. In Great Britain, the counterpart organization is the Governing Council of the Cat Fancy. Many smaller clubs send representatives to meetings of the larger organization to make certain the breeds they represent are given proper consideration. Clubs also maintain files in which purebred cats are registered, their lineage documented.

On the following pages are descriptions of the major breeds of cats that now exist. Precise standards for each breed are not given, as these vary to some degree with the different organizations. The general specifications for a show-quality cat are indicated, however. For example, on a Siamese, judges will consider its "points"—tail, feet and legs, ears, and mask—as **40** well as its coat, eye color, and body and head shape. A person

▲ Silver Tabby

who wants to become involved with cat shows should start attending local events. They are held in every major city and are well announced. From the contacts made at these shows the cat owner can become as involved as he or she wishes.

All organizations divide cats into two basic categories: shorthaired and longhaired. In this book, the breeds of cats are listed alphabetically, irrespective of length of coat. The longhaired cats are generally considered the aristocrats among domestic cats. In Britain, these cats are called "longhairs," while in the U.S.A. and Canada they are generally referred to as "Persians." They were, of course, developed from shorthaired cats. The longhaired feature first appeared as a "sport," or mutant, and was then carefully preserved and developed by breeding. In this manner, too, new breeds appear with regularity. If their features are desirable and the breeders persist, the breed is eventually given recognition, its standards registered. Similarly, long-time favorites decline in popularity as the public's favor shifts.

41

▲ Bi-colored Persians

Abyssinian

Rabbit-cat is another fitting name for the Abyssinian, one of the more distinctive of all the feline breeds, for its short, dense fur is indeed rabbitlike. It occurs in two color varieties: brown and an almost copper red. In both the coat is ticked—that is, each hair banded with several grades of dark and light. In the Brown Abyssinian the fur is usually dark brown to almost black in a line down the center of the back. The pads of the feet are black, and some black also extends up the legs. In the Reds the line down the middle of the back is brownish, the pads of the feet and also the nose are pinkish, and the backs of the legs are brown to mahogany. The body and legs have no other outstanding marks. Some have a white chin, but this is not an allowable feature in show cats. Both Blue and Cream Abyssinians have been developed, but they are very rare.

Though the origin of the Abyssianian is still disputed, most authorities believe the breed is ancient and that it is the Abyssinian, in fact, that is depicted in the art and sculpture of ancient Egypt. It is in all probability the sacred cat of Egypt. Why is it called Abyssinian? The first of these cats taken to Europe were obtained in Abyssinia (now Ethiopia).

Abyssinians are lovable cats and quite devoted to their owners, some so much so that their loyalty is to one person only. They tend to respond to training more slowly than some other breeds, but they learn well. If the owner persists, an Abyssinian can be taught to retrieve balls and do other simple tricks. If accustomed to a leash an Abyssinian will not object to it. Nor does the adult lose its kittenish playfulness.

Long and slim-bodied, the Abyssinian is graceful, with a long and distinctly tapered tail. Its head is triangular or wedge-shaped, the ears noticeably large and pointed. Eye color ranges from green to hazel or yellow. Extremely alert and intelligent, the Abyssinian is also quite vocal, though less so than the Siamese. Its voice is cooing, and rather more comforting than abrasive. Abyssinians are not common, partly because they have small litters (rarely more than four) in which most are **42** males. This also makes them among the most expensive cats.

Abyssinian ▲ Somali (Longhaired Abyssinian) ▲ Abyssinian ▼

Balinese

The long, silky coat of the Balinese has the same basic fawn color as the Siamese, which it also matches with dark brown to black legs, tail, face, and ears. Similarly, too, the eyes are a deep blue. This resemblance is not surprising, for the Balinese first appeared as a mutant in a litter of Siamese in the mid-1950s. This cat was later bred to other longhairs that showed up in subsequent litters, and the offspring of these bred true. From these, seal points, blue points, and chocolate points have been developed, again duplicating the shorthaired Siamese.

The head of the Balinese is wedge-shaped, though a little less so than in the Siamese. The sharpness of the feature is somewhat obscured by the long hair. The ears are wide set and relatively large compared to those of longhaired Persians. The coat is long but not as long as a Persian's and thus needs somewhat less grooming. Like the Siamese, these are affectionate and highly intelligent cats. They do have loud, demanding voices but use them a little less persistently than Siamese.

44

▲ Seal Point Balinese

45

▲ Balinese kitten

Birman

This is the sacred cat of Burma, said to be a descendant of the cats that were kept in Buddhist temples in ancient times. According to the legends, a white longhaired temple cat was a particular priest's intermediary with the gods. The two mediated together in the temple until one day the priest was killed by invaders. The faithful cat remained with the body, all four paws upon its dead master. Suddenly its white coat took on a golden sheen, its yellow eyes changed to blue, and its tail, legs, nose, and ears became earth brown. But its four paws, still resting on the priest, remained pure white, as they are today. All temple

▲ Blue Point Birmans

cats thenceforward were of the same kind, and the death of each cat symbolizes the rise of a priest's soul to heaven. For many years this breed was protected by the priests in Burma. Only recently has it become well known in other countries.

The Birman has a lpng, rather thick body and short, stout legs. The head is wide, the cheeks are full, and the tail is long and full but not bushy. While the basic color is like the Siamese, Birmans have also been bred in a variety of color points: chocolate, seal, blue, and lilac. The Birman is an affectionate cat and is rapidly gaining in popularity.

Black Persian or Longhair

Although one of the oldest of the longhair breeds, the Black Persian has never been common. In fact, it has declined in popularity in recent years. A well-groomed, healthy Black Persian is one of the most striking of cats, but it is difficult to keep in prime condition. For this reason Black Persians are never shown in great numbers. If the cats are allowed outdoors, for example, their coats quickly acquire a yellowish or rusty cast. They must be kept indoors and their coats groomed regularly. Black Persians are not favorites of breeders because litters frequently contain variations in color rather than all blacks. Even all-black kittens generally start with brownish or rusty coats that do not turn fully black until the cat is more than a year old. Any traces of white will disqualify a show cat.

Why these beautiful cats are not more popular as pets is not easily explained. Black cats are traditionally symbols of bad luck, but such superstitions are unlikely to impress—or upset—cat fanciers. Whatever their current standing, long-haired blacks, with their large orange-yellow eyes and solemn stares can be most disarming, and no one can deny that a Black Persian in show condition is one of the most eye-catching of all the breeds of cat.

Black Shorthair

Black Shorthairs share the features of Black Persians but have short, glossy coats. In many the eyes are green, but for show they must be orange, or copper. Like Black Persians, they must be pure black, even their lips, nose, and foot pads.

Most Black Shorthairs cannot qualify for shows, because however well qualified otherwise, they have white chins, collars, or spots somewhere on the body. As in Black Persians, the breeding of pure-black shorthairs is very difficult, and the breeder must wait until the kittens are at least a year old before he can be certain that the desired color will remain constant. The kittens are usually rusty in color or have tabby markings.

Blue-cream Persian or Longhair

This is a controversial breed because its color is sex-linked, and with rare exceptions only females are known. If males are born, they usually do not live long. For show acceptability in Great Britain the blue and cream hairs in the coat must be evenly intermingled. In United States shows the coat must have patches of blue and cream. This breed, the result of crossing a Blue and a Cream, has a long, soft coat and coppery or orange eyes. Many have a blaze of cream on the forehead. Though not common, particularly because of the breeding problems, the Blue-cream Longhair is certainly one of the attractive longhaired cats. **51**

Blue-cream Shorthair

This is the shorthaired counterpart of the Blue-cream Persian. Similarly, almost all are females. The few males that do survive are sterile. The breed is produced by mating a shorthaired Blue with a shorthaired Cream. As in the longhaired breed, the British show regulations call for a totally "misty" coat—a complete mingling of the two shades. In the United States the coat must have patches of the two colors. In both the coat must be soft, never coarse or wiry. The eyes may be coppery or orange. Green is not accepted for shows.

This attractive breed also makes an excellent and devoted pet, not uncommonly becoming attached to a particular member of the household almost to the exclusion of others. It has the unusual habit of dipping or scooping its food from its bowl with its paw, and also prefers drinking from a dripping hose or faucet to drinking from a bowl. A litter produced by a Blue-cream can be a surprise of color combinations because of the female's genetic mixture.

Blue Persian or Longhair

Among cat fanciers this is the most popular of all the longhaired breeds. In show cats the coat must be uniform in color, but any shade of blue is accepted. Most breeders work for the paler tone, which gives the cats a nearly lilac hue. Deeper shades, almost lavender, also occur. In nonshow cats it is not uncommon for the coat to be spotted with white on the underside. For show the eyes must be orange or coppery. Yellow and green eyes occur regularly in the breed. All have a prominent neck ruff that frames the wide head. The ears are small. Some have been bred to have very short noses, so that they have an almost Pekingese appearance, but accompanying this is the feature of running or "weeping" eyes, not desirable for show purposes.

The Blue Longhair or Blue Persian is often used in breeding to maintain or to improve the standards of other longhaired cats. It is difficult, therefore, to be sure of the genetic purity of two blue parents. The litter they produce may not contain any blues at all, or occasionally a blue will appear in a litter of tabbies or other nonblue parents.

Burmese

Burmese cats did not originate in Burma. The breed was established in the United States in the 1930s by breeding a brown cat from Burma with a Siamese, and then continuing the breeding of the offspring. The Siamese lineage is still evident, but the Burmese is a much stockier cat, the coat almost velvety soft. The ears are large, though not as large as those of the Siamese. The Burmese has a wedge-shaped or triangular head, and the yellow to gold eyes are almond-shaped. Its slim tail has a bend near the tip. The feet are small, almost dainty in comparison to the body.

The basic color of the original Burmese is dark brown, gradually becoming lighter on the belly. For show cats no white should show on the body, but the legs, face mask, and ears may be a richer seal brown. Kittens are typically much lighter, with a hint of tabby shades, but usually become dark by the time they are a year old. In Great Britain breeders work toward slimmer, longer-bodied cats, which are favored in shows. In the United States a sturdier, more compact body is preferred, the head more blunt or rounded.

Blue Burmese have blue-gray fur. They were developed in the mid-1950s and became a recognized color variety in about 1960. The fur is distinctly darker to almost black down the middle of the back, becoming lighter on the chest and belly. Kittens are light in color, some showing tabby markings.

Still other color variations are being developed so that they breed true. These include red, champagne (chocolate), cream, blue-cream, platinum (lilac), and others. The attention given the Burmese is the result of the breed's popularity as a pet as well as for shows. Burmese kittens are almost unbelievably active and agile. They slow down considerably when they mature, becoming affectionate and quite loyal, but regularly involving themselves in the unexpected to command attention. They vocalize often, somtimes seeming almost to be muttering to themselves.

They are not as obtrusive as Siamese.

▲ Champagne Burmese ▼ Dark and Champagne Burmese kittens

British Blue

The most popular of the shorthaired breeds in Great Britain is the British Blue, a well-proportioned cat, its head, tail, and legs conforming in size and sturdiness to its rather sturdy body. The eyes of cats bred for show are deep orange or coppery and the coat is uniformly blue-gray. In addition to their popularity for shows the British Blues are liked simply as pets. They are loyal, affectionate, and mild-mannered.

The Chartreux, of France, is very similar but usually a bit stockier, the head somewhat rounder, and the jaws more powerful. In many the coat tends toward being woolly.

In American shows these cats are classed as Exotic Shorthairs, a category for all shorthaired complements of the longhaired or **56** Persian breeds.

Cameo Persian or Longhair

Several color varieties of this exotic longhaired breed now occur. Palest is the Shell Cameo, which has a very white undercoat and pale pink to peachlike ticking on the fur. The Red Smoke also has a white undercoat, but the hairs are more deeply tipped with red. The tips of the ears and the ruff are white. In between these two is the Shaded Cameo, whose undercoat is white but with the reddish ticking fading to white on the belly, chest, and chin. The Cameo Tabby has an off-white undercoat and is marked with red above. In all color variations the eyes are coppery, but they are deepest, almost gold, in the Red Smoke. The nose is pink and the eyes are lined with pink. This is still an experimental breed, but it is growing in popularity because of its attractiveness.

▲ Shell Cameo Persian

Chinchilla

Sometimes referred to as Silver, this is one of the most photo-genic breeds of cats, appearing often in advertisements where both beauty and daintiness are sought. Compared to other long-haired breeds, the Chinchilla tends to be delicate. Its coat is pure white, each hair tipped with black to give it a silvery appear-ance. The medium-length tail is almost bushy and the fur on the chest and neck are shaggy. The tip of the nose is red, the eyes are emerald green, the lids lined with black. The pads of the feet are also black. Keeping these exquisitely beautiful cats in prime condition for show requires effort. The long coat tends to yel-low, especially around the tail. Owners often keep their coats well powdered, to help absorb the oil that accumulates in the coat and causes matting.

Kittens commonly have a banded tail, but the bands usually disappear before maturity. Some are born with dark bands on their legs; these persist, making the cats no good for show purposes.

Varieties include the Shaded Silver, whose ticking is much darker and whose undercoat is off-white rather than pure white. In the Masked Silver the face and paws are black. Another variety is the Blue Chinchilla. Its basic color is bluish, the fur ticked with steel gray on the tail, back, sides, and head. Its eyes are orange, unlike the green eyes of other Chinchillas.

▲ Shaded Silver. ▼ Chinchilla

Cream Persian or Longhair

Purity of color is difficult to maintain with the Cream Persian, which apparently originated from a cross of Blue and Red longhaired cats. The color in a show cat must be pale cream, with no blotched markings (common in kittens) and no pure white. The coat should not be ticked. Each hair should be solid in color to its roots. The large round eyes are copper or deep orange. There is a tendency for the coat to become woolly. In show cats it must be silky.

Cream Shorthair

This is one of the oldest breeds among show cats, but it is nevertheless rare because breeders have great difficulty in maintaining the purity of color required for show. Kittens are commonly marked with bands of darker color on the tail, legs, and face, but if these do not disappear by the time the kitten is about two months old they will remain throughout the animal's life, disqualifying it for exhibition purposes. The eyes are coppery gold.

Cream Shorthairs are even-tempered and make excellent pets. Those with defects that eliminate them from shows are still handsome enough to earn admiring comments.

▲ Cream Persians ▼ Cream Shorthair

61

Egyptian Mau

The Egyptian Mau is still not officially recognized, but it is accepted for exhibition by most cat organizations. Long and lithe, with a wedge-shaped head, the Mau bears close resemblance to cats shown in Egyptian paintings. The tail is long and tapered, the eyes are almond-shaped. In one color variety, known as the Silver Mau, the background is silvery, with black spots and bars over the body. In another, the Bronze Mau, the **62** coat is marked with bronze bars and splotches.

▲ Silver Mau (left) and Bronze Mau (right)

Havana

Originally called Chestnut Brown and often referred to as Havana Brown, this new breed was first recognized in the late 1950s and is still being developed. It did not originate in Cuba. It was named for its color—rich cigar tobacco brown. The popularity of the Havana is growing, both for shows and as pets. It is a responsive, intelligent, and affectionate cat with a quiet, sophisticated manner—winning ways that foretell a bright future for the breed.

The Havana has a complex heritage dominated by Siamese and Burmese breeds. It resembles a Burmese, in fact, but has slanted green eyes, rather than gold as in the Burmese. The short, glossy coat is brighter than the coat of the Burmese. The pink pads on its feet are also distinctive. In show cats no black is allowable in the coat. The muzzle is sharp, as in the Siamese, and the head well proportioned on the long, lithe body. The tail is slim and whiplike.

Himalayan or Longhaired Colorpoint

The striking Himalayan, produced by breeding the Siamese with several longhaired breeds over a number of generations, has been a recognized breed only since the 1950s, becoming highly popular in its short existence. It appears regularly in shows, but is also desirable as a pet because of its warm, affectionate personality. In length of coat and body shape the Himalayan has the characteristics of a Persian, but in colors it shows its Siamese heritage distinctly. Color varieties include seal point, blue, chocolate, lilac, tortie, and red. The blue eyes are round, matching those of the Siamese but less intense. Lost in the breeding, too, is the loud, demanding voice of the Siamese, another feature favoring the Himalayan. Kittens are pale, their colors developing with maturity.

▲ Flame, or Red, Point Himalayan

▲ Seal Point Himalayan ▼ Seal Point kitten

Japanese Bobtail

Known in the United States for less than a decade, the Japanese Bobtail has been a familiar breed in Japan for many centuries. It has a stump tail about two to four inches long, in this respect resembling some of the short-tailed Manx cats (to which it is not related). Like the Manx, its hind legs are longer than its front legs; the ears are large, the head is long. It occurs in a wide range of solid and mixed colors.

Korat

The Korat got its start in the United States when a pair of these handsome silvery blue cats were imported in 1959. Although still-rare and expensive, they are growing in popularity. The breed was recognized in the mid-1960s. Even the history of the breed in its native Thailand is obscure, but there is evidence that it played a role in the development of the blue point Siamese.

Medium-sized and muscular, the Korat has dense, soft fur. Its large, greenish-gold eyes are an outstanding feature. The face is heart-shaped, the muzzle sharp but not pointed. The ears are large, their tips rounded. The blunt-tipped tail is medium length.

In addition to being a show cat, the Korat, meaning "silver" in Thailand, has gained great favor as a pet because it is affectionate and responds well to training. Korats can be taught simple tricks, seeming to derive pleasure from their performances. **67**

Maine Coon Cat

No one knows the precise origin of the Coon Cat, but it is believed that the breed stems from indeterminate longhaired cats brought to the United States by sailors. Either released or escaped, the cats mated with resident shorthaired cats, and over many generations evolved the Maine Coon Cat. It is a powerfully built cat with hair of medium length—that is, not as long as in Persians. The coat does not become matted or tangled as readily as in those with longer hair, which makes grooming easier. But the most striking feature of the coat is its resemblance to a raccoon's. This gave rise to the name Coon Cat and also to the mistaken belief that these cats resulted from crossbreeding with raccoons, a biological impossibility.

Maine Coon Cats have long been popular as pets locally and were commonly neutered. This kept their numbers at a rather stable low level. In recent years they have begun to appear in shows, and standards for their acceptance have been established. Coon Cats have big heads, large ears, and yellowish oval eyes. They wear a prominent ruff, a protective feature in the cold Maine climate, and have a medium-length bushy tail. In addition to the raccoon pattern, they occur in a range of solid and mixed colors. The males are exceptionally large, weighing as much as 40 pounds (18.2 kg); females may weigh 25 pounds (11.4 kg). In addition to being handsome, these big cats earn their keep by catching rats and mice.

Manx

The Manx is a tailless cat, with only a hollow to indicate where the tail would fit if it existed. A popular nickname is "Rumpy." A litter occasionally contains kittens with tails several inches long. These cats are referred to as "Stumpies."

The origin of the Manx is obscure. It is conjectured that it arose as a mutant from cats living on the Isle of Man. The tailless condition was evidently dominant, as are most mutations, and so it persisted in the island's isolation until tailed cats were excluded. The breeding of Manx cats on the Isle of Man is a profitable business today.

The Manx stirs up conversation because of its many rabbitlike features. Some people are convinced, in fact, that the Manx is a cross between a rabbit and a cat. This is not possible, of course, but some of the features are startlingly comparable. Because the Manx's hind legs are considerably larger and more powerful than its front legs, it has a rabbitlike appearance. It tends to hop like a rabbit, is a high jumper, and can run fast. It occurs in all colors and mixtures; the fur is soft and dense, much like a rabbit's. The Manx has a large head in comparison to the size of its body, and its medium-sized, wide-spaced ears have pointed tips.

The unusual features of the Manx make it much in demand as a pet. Owners soon learn, however, to love their animals as a soft-voiced, affectionate, and intelligent companion.

Rex

The Rex is a novelty breed, its short, curly coat also earning it the name of Poodle Cat. Even its whiskers are curly. Genetically this is a dominant characteristic, and so the dense, wavy coat may appear in litters of any cats with Rex in their breeding. The Rex first appeared in 1950 and is named for the Rex rabbit that has a similar kind of coat. Because of its rarity, the Rex remains quite expensive.

An affectionate cat, the Rex makes an excellent pet and responds well to training. It is becoming popular with those who are disturbed by the constant shedding of the longhaired breeds but do not like straight, short hair. The Rex has a long, slim body, commonly carrying its back arched. The head is wedge-shaped, the ears are large and the eyes almond-shaped. The tail is long and tapered, the legs long and straight. The Rex occurs in all solid and mixed colors for cats. Two similar but distinct types are recognized: Cornish Rex, which was first to be recognized; and Devon Rex, which did not appear until 1960. When these two are mated their offspring have straight coats.

▼ Black Rex ▲ Cornish Rex ▼ Tabby Rex

Red Self

No longer as popular as in the past, the Red Self is nevertheless a quite attractive breed. It is an English specialty that reproduces only its own color. Its rarity can be at least partly attributed to the difficulty in achieving a pure coat. For show the soft, silky fur must be a rich reddish orange, completely lacking tabby markings. The breed was developed from the Red Tabby, however, and so these marks do appear regularly on the head and tail, a matter of no great concern if the cat is kept as a pet. The eyes are large and coppery, matching the coat, and the lips and nose are pinkish. The ears are small and pointed. Varieties with lighter coats have been developed from the Red Self stock. The Peke-faced Red is identical, except that it has a very pug or depressed nose, sometimes less protruding than the eyes.

Russian Blue

The Russian Blue is another breed of obscure ancestry, but the thick fur suggests that the development took place in a cold climate where a coat of this density would be needed for warmth. The outer coat stands up stiffly but is also short and thick. Sleek and graceful, the Russian Blue's coat is slate blue to an almost lavender shade, the color uniform over the entire body in show cats. The oval eyes are bright green; the pointed ears are thin-skinned, almost transparent. Because of the narrow, flat skull, the forehead recedes. The neck is noticeably long.

Agile, the Russian Blue is active if given an opportunity, preferring the outdoors but also adapting to sedentary apartment life. Even-tempered, affectionate, and intelligent, the Russian Blue is normally silent. It is one of the few breeds that allows itself to be led on a leash. It is generally aloof to strangers. **75**

Scottish Fold

Known only since the early 1960s, the Scottish Fold originated in Scotland. It is a shorthaired cat occuring in a wide variety of colors and patterns but is distinguished by its short ears that fold forward and lie against the top of the head. This is another unusual "sport" that has captured the attention of breeders sufficiently to continue the breed—at least for now. The Scottish Fold is not yet recognized by cat fanciers' associations as a standard.

Seal Point Siamese ▶

Siamese

This is the "royal cat of Siam," truly the aristocrat of all the shorthaired cats. It became immediately popular when it was introduced to the United States and Europe in the late 1800s. Among pedigreed cats, the Siamese is now the most common.

The classic Siamese of today—greatly changed by breeding from the round-faced types first introduced—is a well-proportioned animal, with a long, slender body and slim legs. The tail is long and tapered to a point, some individuals retaining the kink near the tip that was characteristic of the cats originally. The head is triangular, as are the large, wide-based, pointed ears. In all varieties the almond-shaped eyes are bright blue. In some the eyes are crossed, another holdover feature. The short coat is glossy and fine-textured. Kittens are born all

white, their colors not developing until they are two or three months old. Numerous colors have been developed as breeders work to produce varieties they feel will appeal to the public. The most commonly seen are:

Seal Point, the most prevalent, is cream to light brown or fawn over most of the body. The points—tail, feet and legs, ears, and mask—are dark brown.

Blue Point is white over most of its body, grading to bluish on the back. The tail, feet and legs, ears, and mask are bluish.

Chocolate Points are said to be among the first to leave Siam and win the attentions of early cat fanciers. Body color should be ivory with points the color of milk chocolate.

Frost (Lilac) Point has an off-white body, grading into pinkish gray on the tail, feet and legs, ears and mask.

78   Tabby Point, or Lynx Point, is the result of crossing the

▲ Tortie Point Siamese

▲ Lilac Point kittens ▼ Lilac Point Siamese

▲ Blue Point

▲ Chocolate Point ▼ Blue Point

Siamese with tabbies. The recognized show-acceptable Tabby Point has ears of a solid color, bearing a thumbprint mark but no stripes. The mask is striped, and the whisker pads are prominently dotted. The legs have broken stripes, the markings solid on the rear of the hind legs. The tail is distinctly ringed, the tip solid.

Red Point has a white body, grading to a light red-orange on the back. The tail, legs and feet, ears, and mask are a bright reddish orange.

Tortie Point, always a female, has tortoiseshell markings on the points. The body is cream or fawn.

Siamese are acknowledged to be the most doglike of the cats. They are highly intelligent and responsive to training. They accept being led on a leash and most seem also to enjoy traveling in an automobile. Their most objectionable feature is their hoarse, piercing voice—and if a normal tone does not achieve their desires they howl loudly. As with all cats, of course, each individual has a distinctive personality, but almost all Siamese are very talkative.

82

▲ Lynx, or Tabby, Point

▲ Lynx, or Tabby, Point ▼ Red Point

Smoke Persian or Longhair

One of the most strikingly colored of all cats, the Smoke Persian has a jet black coat with each hair grading to silver at its roots. As the cat walks the white shows through. The face, ears, and legs are intensely black, but the ruff, ear tufts, face frill, and skirt along the sides of the body are silvery. The tail is a mixture of black and silver hairs. The large, round eyes are copper. Kittens are all black at birth, the full color not appearing until they are several months old. As with all longhaired cats, the Smoke must be groomed regularly to keep its coat in good condition.

The Blue Smoke is a lighter version in which the black is replaced with blue. It is handsome but less impressive than the Smoke Persian. Both are much less popular now than they were half a century ago. A shorthaired Smoke, with a coat of black-tipped white hairs, has also been developed.

▲ Smoke Persian ▼ Blue Smoke Persian

Sphinx (Hairless) Cat

Unquestionably the least handsome of cats, the Sphinx was preserved originally as a novelty, having appeared as a mutant. It is now frequently exhibited in shows, always commanding attention and comment. Kittens are born with a light covering of normal-length hair, but this disappears before they are weaned. The adult's body is covered with very short, dense hair that has the feeling of suede. In many places the skin shows through. The Sphinx has no whiskers. Its eyes are gold, and its tail is long and whiplike.

Because it lacks the protective coat of the normal cat, the Sphinx prefers warm weather, or it must be kept indoors and away from drafts to prevent it from catching cold. The cat, like the duckling, is oblivious to its ugliness and seems to be more sociable and affectionate than many other breeds.

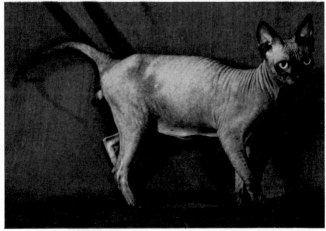

▲ Sphinx Cat

Tabby Persian or Longhair

Tabby Persians have the identical markings of Tabby Shorthairs, differing only in the length of the long, silky hair. Their markings include distinctive lines or pencil marks on the head, swirled around the eyes and the cheeks. Three prominent dark stripes extend the length of the back and two cross the chest. The sides bear vertical bars and swirls, and on the thighs they become horizontal. The legs have dark bracelets. The tail is ringed.

All Tabby Persians conform in basic body structure—that is, they are rather massively built but well proportioned. The legs are short and thick, the tail is short and fully furred or brushlike (as wide as the body when brushed and spread out). The head is wide and round, the nose pug, and the small ears are wide set, almost hidden in fur.

Principal color varieties are listed here. Others have been **87**

▲ Silver Tabby Persian

▲ Brown Tabby Persian

developed, but all are difficult to maintain in show-quality standards because of a strong tendency to revert to features — such as a long tail or larger and pointed ears —tracing to their shorthaired heritage. Kittens do not achieve their full coloration until several months after birth. Tabby Persians make good pets, but their owners must be prepared to give them the additional care that is demanded by their long coats and to tolerate a degree of hair resulting from normal shedding.

Blue Tabby Persian is pale bluish with fawn overtones. Even the lips and chin are bluish. The tabby markings are a much deeper blue. The eyes are orange to copper.

Brown Tabby Persian is an old variety not commonly seen. The background color is a tawny sable and the markings are an intense black. The large, round eyes must be copper or deep orange in show cats, but green eyes are common in the variety. In some the chin and the tip of the tail are white, but this is not allowed in show cats.

Cameo Tabby has a pale cream background color and the tabby markings are beige or reddish. The eyes are coppery gold.

Red Tabby has a rich red basic coat color with even darker red tabby markings. The large, round, copper eyes are set in a broad head and the nose is blunt. White commonly appears on the chest, chin, and tail and disqualifies a cat for shows.

Silver Tabby is pale silver with intensely black markings. The eyes are hazel or green. The popularity of the Silver Tabby has diminished since the development of the Chinchilla. **89**

▲ Red Tabby Persian

Tabby Shorthair

Most common house and alley cats are "tabbies," or at least have the breed somewhere in their undocumented family histories. The breed is old, having originated in the Attabiah district of Bagdad, where Jewish weavers copied the varied colors of their common cats in making a popular silk pattern that was sold widely in Europe. The silk was sold under the name of "tabbi" —hence the name of the cat.

Tabbies with pedigrees are not common. They must conform to rather strict patterns, as described for Tabby Persians, but the latitude in eye color and other features is broader than for most breeds. Shorthairs differ from the longhairs not only in the length of the hair but also in body form. Their legs and tail are longer. The head is broad and the eyes are wide set, but the muzzle is not greatly shortened. The ears are widely spaced and medium-sized rather than small. Similarly, the neck is medium in length and in good proportion to the size of the body. The tail is rather

▲ Striped Tabby Shorthair

▲ Striped Tabby Shorthairs ▼

thick at the base and tapers to a point. The short coat is neat, often becoming thicker in winter.

Tabby Shorthairs occur in the same color varieties as Tabby Persians. Some go by several different names. The Brown Tabby, for example, is sometimes called Blotched Tabby or Marbled Tabby, while the Red is known also as Orange Tabby. Most common in shows is probably the striking Silver Tabby. The familiar Striped or Tiger Tabby has a gray background color with narrow, tigerlike vertical black stripes from the shoulder to the tail. Its eyes are green.

Tabbies make excellent pets. They have no special features that set them apart in habits or personality. They are simply classic examples of cats in all respects.

▲ Mackeral Tabby

▲ Red Tabby Shorthair ▼ Silver Tabby Shorthair

Tortoiseshell Persian or Longhair

In color and pattern, the Tortoiseshell Longhair duplicates the Tortoiseshell Shorthair. In show cats, too, the patches of red, black, and cream in the long, silky coat must not mix or fade into each other. The body is more massive, however, the legs are shorter and the nose is pug. Almost all are females. The few males that do occur are, with rare exceptions, sterile. This, of course, makes the breeding to maintain the standards extremely difficult. The female must be mated with a male of a solid color, and often no tortoiseshells occur in the litter produced.

The Tortoiseshell-and-white Longhair is the complement of the shorthaired variation and goes also by the name of Calico Cat.

▲ Tortoiseshell Persian

▲ Tortoiseshell Persian ▼ Calico Longhair

Tortoiseshell Shorthair

One of the oldest breeds of cats, though not currently ranking high in popularity, the Tortoiseshell Shorthair demands a minimum of grooming in show cats and is also an excellent house pet. Nearly all are females. Males are a rarity and are usually sterile. For shows, the patches of red, black, and cream must be evenly distributed over the body and must not intermingle. The large, round eyes can be hazel, copper, or orange, and a blaze of red down the center of the face is preferred. Tortoiseshells are not easily bred to fit the standards, particularly since there are no males. Tabby markings and white hair are common faults.

The Tortoiseshell-and-white Shorthair, also called Calico Cat, differs from the regular Tortoiseshell Shorthair only in having white on its face, chest, and legs. This variation is, in fact, the most popular.

▲ Tortoiseshell Shorthair

▼ Calico Shorthairs ▲

White Shorthair

White Shorthairs are really rare. The color is easily lost in crossbreeding. Those exhibited in shows must be pure white (not a single hair of another color), and they must have a pink nose. Most show standards require blue eyes, but yellow or green eyes, which are more common, are acceptable in some. Deafness occurs regularly in the blue-eyed White Shorthair, as it does in the White Persian. In both cases, breeders are convinced that this problem can be eliminated in time by selective breeding. Like other shorthaired breeds, the White Shorthair must have a broad head, a medium-length muzzle, and small ears. The body is sturdy and muscular, the legs are well proportioned, and the medium-length tail is thick at the base and tapered.

While black cats are usually considered omens of bad luck and white signify good luck, the reverse is true in some countries—that is, the white cat is looked upon as a sign of bad luck.

Copper-eyed White Persian ▶

White Persian or Longhair

A long white coat identifies the White Persian, which varies otherwise only in the color of its eyes. Orange and blue eyes are accepted for shows, and some have one blue and one orange eye. Green-eyed White Persians also occur.

The first longhaired white cats known in Europe came from Angora (now Ankara), the capital of Turkey. They were blue-eyed or had one blue and one orange eye. Later it was disputed whether these Angoras were really different from the White Persians that arrived in Europe somewhat later and not from Turkey. The Angoras did have noticeably softer, silkier fur. Recently the Angora has been rediscovered, so to speak, and may be given recognition with separate standards.

A breed called the Turkish, also a recent introduction, gives

credence to the Angora story. Also from Turkey, the Turkish is all white except for apricot or orange marks on its head and its totally apricot or orange-ish tail, ringed with a darker, almost red color. The Turkish and the Angora differ from the ordinary Persians, too, in having smaller, wedge-shaped heads and larger ears. The eyes of the Turkish are amber.

White cats with blue eyes are frequently deaf, a genetic link occurring between eye color and hearing. Owners of deaf cats sometimes put tags on them so that people will be considerate if the cat does not respond to noises or calls.

All longhaired cats require regular and careful grooming to keep their coats in good condition, particularly white cats. Those that live in the city are likely to become dingy, but all white cats tend to yellow. The cats clean themselves constantly, of course, but they need help. Few cats like soap and water, and it is also not advisable to get them wet in cool or cold weather. A **100** dry bath is recommended (see pp. 136-137).

▼ White Persian ▲ Angora kittens

101

Show Time

At cat shows, champions defend their titles and earn more, new breeds are displayed, and cat lovers have the pleasure of seeing the most handsome and well-groomed examples of all cats. Fall and winter are the traditional times for cat shows, for at this time of year cats' coats are in their prime. Local clubs may schedule shows at almost any time of the year, however, sometimes staging the events so that they do not conflict with but serve more or less as primaries for larger regional and national shows.

The major cat shows are listed in pet magazines and local ones are announced in newspapers. Calendars of events can be obtained from the cat fanciers' associations (p. 156).

If you own a pedigreed cat, you may want to enter it in a show—out of pride or to satisfy yourself that you do indeed have a winner. Whatever the breed, you will probably find the competition stiff—your cat appraised against the best in the area or in the nation—but win or lose, you will find the experience rewarding. Cat owners have much to share, and at every show you will learn. **103**

▲ Judging at a cat show ▼ Decorated cage

But before you become an exhibitor and enter your cat in a show, it is best to attend one or more events strictly as a spectator so that you will feel comfortable about what is expected of you and your cat. Though there are some differences in the regulations of different organizations and also in specialty events, all cat shows are basically alike.

You must register your cat well in advance of the actual show—usually several weeks. This includes paying an entry fee and filing registration forms that give your cat's history. If this is not a first-time appearance, you will also indicate the specifics of any previous winnings. On the day of the show, each cat entered is given a careful inspection by a veterinarian to make certain that it does not have fleas or other medical reasons for disqualification. The veterinarian will reject an entrant if there is the slightest doubt about the animal, for he or she is responsible not only for that particular cat but for the well-being of the others in the show. Owners are equally concerned about the exposure of their animals to other cats, and they usually do a personal job of cleaning up and disinfecting the holding cage in which their cat will wait until time for it to be judged.

The holding cages are in rows in the exhibit area. In some shows, particularly those in Great Britain, the cat is allowed only a small blanket to lie on plus a litter tray. In most United States shows, the holding cages can be decorated in whatever way the owner elects either to make his cat more comfortable or to give it the best display. At some shows, food is provided—usually by companies that are promoting particular brands of cat food—but most owners prefer to bring the kind of food that satisfies their particular cat's whims. The cages are often kept covered to keep the cats calm and undisturbed by the hubbub. **105**

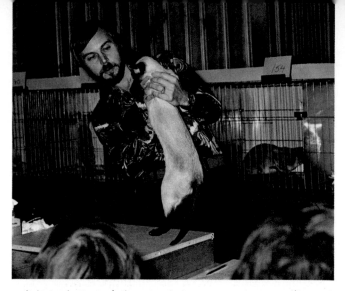

It is against regulations to give nervous cats tranquilizers to keep them soothed until judging time. If there is any indication that a cat has been given drugs, it is immediately disqualified. But the quietness of the cats at a show is truly astonishing. Some breeds, of course, are naturally "talkative" and continue to vent their feelings at shows as they do at home. Most cats accept the situation coolly and quietly, either just tolerating the ordeal or sometimes seeming actually to relish the attention.

Cats are listed in the program by numbers, classed by breed and whatever events they have entered. When a cat's number is called, the owner removes his animal from its holding cage and takes him forward to a special cage with that number on it in the judging area. The cat owners are not permitted to talk to the judges and must, in fact, stay out of the judging area.

In most shows there are four judges. Two of the judges have the special responsibility of the finals for the shorthair and longhair cats; the other two judge the finals in which both shorthair and longhair breeds compete. Each judge has a special table with bright lights for examining coat color and other details. This inspection area is referred to as the "ring." Every animal is given careful inspection. Working down his list of numbers with assistants, a judge examines each cat individually for good health and general appearance, head shape, color of

eyes and coat, and general conformation—that is, body structure and proportion. Cat fanciers' associations have established rigid standards for each of the breeds. Each judge is an expert. He knows all of the breed standards, and he also knows how to handle the cats. Nothing escapes his attention.

Cats may be entered in one or several different show classes. The *championship class* is for cats of either sex eight months or older and in an officially recognized breed. This class is subdivided into *novices,* for cats that have never been ribbon winners in an official or licensed show; *grand champions,* for cats with a number of previous wins; and *alters,* for cats that have been neutered or spayed. The *nonchampionship class* accommodates *kittens,* four to eight months old; *any-other-variety,* for registered cats for which there is no championship classification, usually because of color; and *household pets,* for breeds not recognized by the association licensing the show. In United States shows, the winners in the various classes are awarded ribbons—blue for first, red for second, and yellow for third. In Great Britain, red is first, blue second.

Males and females in the different classes are judged separately, with ribbons awarded for the Best-of-Color (BOC) in the breeds. This may be given either to a male or to a female. Another award is the Best Opposite Sex (BOX) for the best color **107**

in an animal of the opposite sex of the BOC winner. In the final awards, cats with the highest total scores get trophies or other special recognition. Large cat shows may have several thousand entrants. In the United States, these big shows last for two or even three days. In Great Britain, where the show procedures are basically the same but with some differences in classes and in the breeds that are recognized, cat shows are one-day events.

Cat shows confirm that no cat is perfect, but they provide owners with the opportunity to show that their cat is close to it.

Of what benefit are cat shows aside from the personal flattery of having your cat admired and put in the "social register" with the elite? Since the first cat show was held in London's Crystal Palace in 1871, the breeding of cats for show purposes has flourished. The first official cat show in the United States was held in Madison Square Garden in 1895. As a result of these expositions (now several hundred each year), animals with the most desirable features—and cat shows *are* essentially beauty contests—are recognized. By careful selection and breeding of these especially fine specimens, litters are obtained that retain or even accentuate these features. For some people, cat breeding as a hobby evolves into a profession, and visits to major shows become business trips to make certain the standards of particular breeds are maintained and improved while still other breeds are being developed. Participation in cat shows convert a cat's master from a simple pet owner into a fancier dedicated to perfection of the breed. He or she is concerned not only in appearance of the breed but also in health and temperament.

Eventually these benefits are passed on—far beyond the "ring" and the tense moments of judging at the shows—to the cat whose world consists only of its owner's heart and hearth. **109**

From Mating to Motherhood

From one cat to many cats is quick and easy, if you permit it. If you have a female cat she is capable of producing litter after litter. Allowed to prowl, a male will join others now and then in howling, scrapping contests as he vies for the attention of some female in the neighborhood. Many people are really unconcerned about how many cats they are responsible for in the world, or even for the welfare of their own cat. But fortunately you do care.

If you live in an apartment and your cat is accustomed to confinement, you may simply tolerate the periodic sexual urges and wailing. Because your cat is isolated you will not have to worry about parenthood. If your cat is a male, however, you can expect him to spray urine here and there when he is in the mating mood. Don't scold the cat! This is natural behavior, **110** however intolerable to housekeepers. If your cat is a female and

seems to be suffering unduly from unsatisfied desire, your veterinarian can supply a pill to hurry her out of her mood.

No matter where you live, you can curb sexual ardor and prevent unwanted litters by having you male cat neutered, your female spayed. The proper age is about six months for the female, seven for the male. The result is a gentler, calmer, more temperate cat, no longer prone to the urgencies of procreation and the wanderlust to satisfy them. Neutering operations are simple and not expensive, less so for males than for females. If you do not want more cats or the caterwauling that heralds the onset of sexual periods, this is an excellent solution. Yes, an altered cat can gain weight, but you control the diet. The gain is not necessary. If you have waited until the cat is old enough— that is, already sexually mature—there will be no upset in hormone balance to cause an automatic weight problem. Except for its sex desires, a neutered cat is otherwise not changed in personality or behavior. **111**

So You Want More Cats

If your cat is pedigreed, chances are you really want more kittens. They have an established market value, and only a few litters will more than cover your cat's expenses. You may also be interested in crossbreeding to develop particular characteristics. For some people, cat breeding becomes a hobby or even a profession. Your queen, which is the name given the female brood cat, may not have a pedigree, but you want her to have a family anyhow. Perhaps she is especially intelligent, is uncommonly docile, is exceptionally attractive. Whatever the reason, if you want the kittens yourself or have arranged homes for them before they arrive, you will usually have no difficulty convincing her that she has been made for motherhood. She will not even object if you play matchmaker. Doing this will give you an idea of the kind of kittens she will produce.

A female is just out of kittenhood or only about eight months old when she is ready to bear her first litter. Thereafter she is ready to mate twice a year: winter, and spring or early summer. You will have no difficulty knowing the time once you have seen your queen in action. When she wants a mate, she makes her wish obvious by calling loudly and rolling on her back. She will also become very affectionate to you, as if pleading with you to help her find a mate. If you do nothing, her discomfort and her antics will continue for about a week before she calms down, but if you intend her to have kittens, this is the time to introduce the father of the brood to be.

The meeting can be in a room in your home, or you may prefer to take her to your veterinarian or to a kennel. Somebody should be nearby, however, because sometimes the two do not appeal to each other as much as had been hoped. They may

decide to fight rather than to have a family and you must be on hand to separate them. Normally things go as planned, however. Just to be sure, the couple may be brought together for a second encounter a few days later.

Gestation takes nine weeks, give or take a week. Kittens born much earlier than nine weeks will be premature and probably will not survive. Until about ten days prior to giving birth, the expectant mother will go about life much as usual. Then she becomes less active, and you should try to keep her from jumping. Knowing her condition, however, you should make certain her diet is enhanced. If you have doubts about what to feed her, ask your veterinarian to supply you with a recommended diet for a pregnant cat. From the start she will get a bit more food than usual. By the end of her pregnancy she will be eating about twice as much as normally. Give her between-meal snacks and make certain she drinks a lot of milk to supply calcium for building bones. Enrich her usual foods with vitamin and mineral supplements.

As the time nears, your queen will begin looking for a place **113**

where she can give birth to her kittens. You can help. Get a large cardboard box and cut one side down to make it easy for her to get in and out, but leave it high enough so that the little kittens cannot crawl out. Unless you plan to put the box in a closet or some other dark place, leave the top on, so that the box itself is dark inside. Your queen will want privacy. Put several layers of newspapers inside and then let her inspect what you have done. If she approves, she will start shredding the newspapers with her claws to make a nest. You can add more papers until she has the nest built and arranged exactly as she wants it. Later you can cover the papers with old blankets or towels to make the nest even warmer for the kittens.

Your queen will spend most of her last days of pregnancy in this box. At this point she probably feels miserable and may be wondering whether having kittens was a good idea. She may also surprise you and go off into some other closet, in a dark corner, or on a bed to give birth. But if you are there when the time arrives, you can make sure she uses the box that the two of **114** you have worked on to make it just right for the event.

You Play Midwife

Cats have been giving birth to kittens for centuries without human help. Your queen can no doubt manage without you. On the other hand, you can comfort her and give her help if it is needed. Have your midwifery needs ready: a small box lined with a soft cloth or towel, a hot-water bottle filled with body-warm water, and a pair of scissors. If the births are normal, your queen will have four to six kittens within two to three hours. Now and then a queen may continue in labor for as long as ten hours, but whenever there are long intervals between the birth of each kitten there is a chance that something is wrong. If you are concerned you can check with your cat's doctor.

Each kitten comes forth head-first and is encased in a shiny sac, like a clear plastic bag. The mother will immediately slit this sac with her teeth to release the tiny kitten inside. If this is not done the kitten will suffocate. Do not interfere unless you see that the mother is not doing what she should do instinctively, for as soon as the kitten is free of the sac, she will also lick it, a massaging that starts its life processes as a free-living creature. At the same time she should cut the umbilical cord with her teeth. If she does not remove the sac you can do it with your fingers. You can also pinch the umbilical cord in two or cut it with your scissors, which should be sterilized, of course. Make the cut close to the kitten's body, leaving only a one- or two-inch (2.5–5 cm) stub. Pinch both of the cut ends together and hold them for several minutes so that there is a minimum of bleeding.

If the mother has not licked her newborn kitten to get its breathing started, put it in a towel and rub it vigorously but without pressing hard. Sometimes a newborn kitten cannot breathe because of mucus that blocks its respiratory passages. If **115**

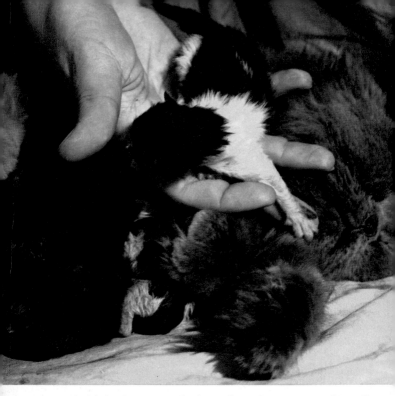

you hold the kitten upside-down for a few minutes, this will drain out.

As each kitten is born put it in the special box with the hot-water bottle. If a kitten cries, put it to one of the mother's teats, from which earlier you have clipped the hair. Following the birth of each kitten, the placenta to which the umbilical cord was attached will also be shed. This is the afterbirth, and it is natural for the mother to eat it. If she does not, remove it anyhow so that it does not interfere with the birth of the next kitten. Keep count of the afterbirths to make sure there is one for each kitten. If one is left inside it can cause an infection. By checking, you may be able to draw it out gently with the umbilical cord.

While your queen is having her kittens, keep a bowl of water nearby so she can get a drink if she wants it. If there is a delay she may even appreciate some milk or a small snack. Giving birth to **116** four, or sometimes as many as eight, kittens is work.

Newborn Kittens

Cats are good mothers, with few exceptions, and for the first few days the new mother generally prefers to take care of her kittens without being bothered. Your cat may tolerate you, but it is best to let her alone. Alley cats often move their kittens a number of times if their hiding places are discovered.

The newborn kittens are blind, their eyelids stuck together by secretions. The eyes do not open for a week or up to 12 days, but even then, the little kittens' eyes do not function properly. They cannot tolerate bright light or see well until they are approaching a month in age. The secretions that hold the eyes tightly shut at first usually soften and go away naturally. If they do not, you may be able to help by cleaning the eyes very gently with moistened cotton. In some cases, a special solution must be used, by your veterinarian, to get the eyes unstuck.

Newborn kittens are also deaf, but their hearing comes to them quickly. They soon learn their mother's language and also respond to their own small voices as they crawl about finding their food.

By the time the kitten is a month old, it has 26 tiny sharp teeth. These are replaced with the larger permanent teeth when the kitten is about six months old, and at the same time 4 more are added to make the total 30. Like human babies, kittens may get out of sorts when their new teeth are erupting through their gums. You can watch this, and if the teeth do not come through properly, you can get help from your veterinarian.

Most important, remember that your young mother was equipped by nature to take care of her offspring. Let her do the work. She expects it and can do it better than you anyhow. Trouble occurs rarely, and that is the only time she needs you. **117**

Room and Board

Two meals a day and a place to sleep. These are the daily needs of the adult cat—most of them, that is. Cats do differ in their demands if not their needs. Some will call for three or more meals a day or as many as they can get. They may prefer smaller amounts more frequently, or they may just be big eaters. Others do well on one meal a day. You will have to work this out with your cat. Remember who is boss in your family. If setting out two meals a day fits your schedule best, stick to it. Your cat can adapt.

For the average cat, about half a pound of food daily is adequate. Most authorities suggest an ounce of food for each pound of weight. Some cats will eat much more if you allow them, and they will get fat, which is really not desirable. Most cat owners feed the big meal in the morning, making the one at night about half as large. This is up to you. Always feed your cat at the same time every day. When the routine is established, it will not be necessary to call your cat at mealtime. It will be waiting and with a good appetite.

As soon as your cat has its fill, it will walk away from the dish and begin cleaning up. Remove the remaining food imme- diately so it will not spoil, smell bad, or also attract insects. If there is much food left, you can save it for the next meal. If you keep it in the refrigerator, warm it to room temperature before serving it. Water should also be available not only at mealtime, but throughout the day. It, too, should be at room temperature.

Make sure your cat's diet is rich in protein. Cats are carnivores—flesh-eaters. They need meat. But meat alone, as **118** we serve it, is not sufficient. A wild cat, for example, eats the

internal organs as well as the flesh of the animals it kills, and in this way it gets the additional minerals and vitamins that are necessary. If you feed fresh meats to your cat, make sure to include organs, such as heart, kidney, and liver, from time to time. Avoid excess fat, trimming the meat if necessary. If you provide fish or chicken, cook it and remove the bones.

Most cats like variety. If you give them the same kind of food day after day, they will eventually reject it. Try something else. Make your cat's meals exciting, but don't let it become choosy. Give it tasty treats occasionally, too. A hardboiled egg, a few pieces of cooked carrot, a boiled potato, some cake with icing. You may be surprised at what appeals to a cat.

If your cat refuses good meals for no reason other than being finicky, insist that it eat what is offered. Let it go hungry, then present the same food again at the next meal. Hunger will win over stubborness. If your cat continues to have no interest in food and is generally listless, it may be ill and should be taken to a veterinarian. But if it is active and its coat has a good sheen, there is no question that it is getting enough of the right kind of food.

Excellent canned and packaged foods, both dry and moist, are available in grocery stores. They are the most convenient, way of getting the proper food for your cat—well-balanced meals that satisfy all the vitamin and mineral needs in good proportion. Most of the kinds on the market today are good, but a few are not. If you have question about a particular brand, ask your veterinarian.

Many cats like milk, too, though some do not. It is best to offer the milk after the meal is eaten. Otherwise your cat may drink

too much and not be able to eat.

Feeding Kittens

A kitten should be kept with its mother until about two months old. At this age it will be weaned—or should be.

If the kitten has been orphaned or must for some other reason be taken from its mother earlier, you will have to do the feeding. Your veterinarian can recommend the best feeding program and will probably prescribe slightly diluted milk to which some minerals and vitamins can be added. If the kitten is still too small to nurse, you will have to get it started. First give it milk with a medicine dropper, but encourage it to suck drops of milk from the tip of your finger or from a milk-soaked cloth. Soon it will be taking milk from a doll's bottle.

How do you know when the kitten has had enough? This is not easily determined. Usually the kitten will simply get tired **121**

and fall asleep, or you may notice bubbles forming at the sides of its mouth, indicating that it is no longer really taking in milk, and when you pull gently on the bottle, there is no sucking pressure to hold it in the kitten's mouth. Do not try to force it to take more. But you must feed the kitten often—at least six times a day.

After each meal, clean the kitten with a washcloth or a sponge moistened with warm water. This will take the place of the licking that the kitten would normally get from its mother. Rub very gently from the head to the rear. This not only helps digestion but also stimulates the bowels to move. Make certain you are holding the kitten over a pan or newspaper so that it does not soil your clothes, bedding, or furniture.

By the time the kitten is eight weeks old, or sometimes earlier, it moves about freely. Its meals will still be mostly milk, but for at least one meal, you can add small amounts of solid foods. Special starter kitten foods can be bought in pet stores, or you can use baby cereal, bits of bread soaked in milk, or even tiny

▲ Spoon feeding

·bits of raw meat scraped from a larger piece with a knife. For most kittens the number of feedings can now be reduced to four, though some will not be satisfied unless they have more. The number of feedings and the amount given each time varies with the kitten. You will have to judge whether the kitten is using all that it eats in growth or is just becoming pot-bellied. In proportion to its weight, it will definitely need more than an adult cat. Remember to keep a bowl of fresh water where the kitten eats.

By the time the kitten is six months old it is losing its kittenish looks. Until now it has added nearly a pound (.45 kg) of weight each month, and for most of this time it has been a soft, roundish ball of fur. Now suddenly it becomes a gangly little cat. Its fat has changed to lean. It requires more food at each feeding—less milk, more solids. The number of feedings can be reduced to two, with maybe a bowl of milk at midday and a snack at bedtime. At eight months the little cat can go on the regular adult feeding schedule.

▲ Bottle feeding

A Place to Sleep

While a kitten is sleeping with its mother it has a warm body to snuggle against—and a place to get a snack is handy, too. If the kitten is orphaned or even after it is weaned, it still needs a warm, soft bed in a place where there are no drafts. You can buy special beds for kittens, or make a box with one side cut low, so the kitten can get in and out easily. You can use a pillow, a mattress from a doll's bed, or spread towels or pieces of blankets. On cool nights fold the covers to make a pocket into which the kitten can crawl to keep warm. Insist that the kitten sleep here.

When the kitten grows up, it may continue to use the same bed—or one like it. As with foods, however, cats do like variety in places to sleep. Your cat may desert its comfortable bed for days at a time to sprawl on a bench or a hearth. It may elect your favorite chair, a counter top in the kitchen or the bathroom, or the top bookshelf. Don't worry about its comfort. Your cat has made the choice itself. Just make certain you approve of the choice, with safety and hygiene in mind. If your cat decides to sleep on a stairstep, for example, it is dangerous both for you and the cat. If it sleeps on a kitchen table or counter top, sanitation may be the issue.

When a cat feels safe in its surroundings, it relaxes completely and sleeps soundly. Sometimes it gets into unbelievable positions, which you can envy but never duplicate. Often the cat is not in a deep sleep, however. It rests with its eyes shut but with its ears tuned to every sound around it. Without opening its eyes it turns its ears to pick up and interpret noises. If disturbed it becomes wide-awake and alert, seeming to size up the situation at once and be ready to spring into action.

Good Habits

Good behavior becomes a habit. To get your cat to behave in an acceptable manner the training must be started when it is a kitten. It is difficult to change an older cat's ways.

Toilet training a kitten is easy. If you live where your cat cannot easily go outdoors, you must provide at least one litter box. Watch the kitten. When it is obviously searching for a place to relieve itself, pick it up immediately and set it either in the litter box or outdoors. Give it a lot of praise when it performs properly. Scold it loudly when it makes a mistake, while at the same time putting it in the litter box or outdoors to let it know where it should have gone. The training will not take long, for cats are naturally particular in their toilet habits. A kitten may learn from its mother about digging a hole in which to defecate and then covering up after itself. If the kitten is alone you may have to show it how by taking a paw in your hand and digging at the litter or dirt, but the kitten will not need more than one or two lessons.

Litter should be changed regularly—immediately after it is used, if possible. From time to time the box should be changed or the pan washed and sterilized. You cat does not like the smell any better than you do.

126   In the wild, cats regularly scratch their claws on the trunks or

▲ Scratching post

branches of trees—not to sharpen the claws, as is often said, but rather to dull them. The claws continue to grow in length just as your fingernails do, and after a while they become uncomfortable for walking on. The scratching wears them down a bit so that they do not catch so easily on objects. Scratching is instinctive, and house cats may turn to furniture, curtains, or other objects in a house. If your cat cannot get outdoors to scratch—and you should be very firm in not allowing the destruction of your furniture—you should provide a scratching place. Special scratching posts can be bought in pet stores, or you can make one by fastening a piece of carpeting to a small log or piece of wood and putting a bit of catnip under the carpet. When your cat starts scratching in the wrong place, take it to the scratching post you have provided. It will appreciate having a special place.

Kittens and even some older cats like playthings. If you do not provide a ball, a rubber mouse, or some similar toys, the kitten will find something else—and usually not what you want it to have. The toys need not be expensive. A kitten can get hours of pleasure from a crumpled piece of cellophane, an empty paper bag, or a cardboard box. Much of a kitten's play can be solitary, but it also enjoys company. This is a good opportunity to solidify your relationship.

Children like to play with kittens, but keep in mind that a kitten tires quickly. After it has played for half an hour or so, let it rest. Soon it will be ready for another session. The interest in playing slackens as the cat gets older, but it is never lost completely. There are times when a cat ten years old or older will suddenly revert to cavorting kittenhood, much to the delight and consternation of those who have watched the cat age. **127**

Belling the Cat

Cats that catch mice and rats are applauded, even encouraged into encores. Those that kill birds are condemned. But to a cat, fur and feathers are equated.

By instinct, all cats are hunters. Even the well-fed cat cannot resist the opportunity to pursue almost any small animal that moves. Any scurrying or rustling attracts a cat's attention and focuses it on potential prey. For some cats, hunting is a pleasurable pastime, and they become skilled at winning their game, partly the result of quiet persistence. Making the catch is sport, but what happens afterward is most disturbing to humans. Unless the cat is ravenously hungry and depends on hunting for its regular meals, it does not kill its catch immediately. Rather it continues to play, tormenting its victim by allowing it to struggle free and then capturing it again. The victim is a living toy but doomed to die, for allowed to continue its way, the cat will keep up the torture until the hapless creature finally succumbs. Then, in most instances, your proud cat will deliver its prize to your doorstep or even bring it indoors to present as a gift. It will never understand your lack of appreciation for these grisly tokens, and by this time, too, the deed is done, making reprimands pointless and misunderstood.

In their defense, very few cats are skilled when it comes to killing birds. Most birds are too fast and too wary to be caught. Researchers point out that the diets even of feral cats that depend on their hunting skill for survival consist of a very low percentage of birds. Perhaps the easiest victims are baby birds in a nest, but most mother birds set up such a ruckus that a cat becomes discouraged and turns to something easier. If your cat

seems to have developed a sudden and uncontrollable craving

to demonstrate its prowess as a bird killer, what can you do? Consider adding a tinkling bell to your cat's collar. The jingling is usually enough to warn birds to be on their way. And without a victory, your cat will eventually give up and be satisfied with the meals you provide for free and with the toys you offer to take the place of the live ones. Cats are not stupid. When they have a choice, they will select the sure thing.

If you see your cat stalking a bird, give it a sharp "No!" or whatever word and tone you use for scolding when your cat misbehaves in other ways. Even though your cat seems to be ignoring you, it will understand the message. With the proper upbringing you have given it, your cat knows right from wrong and will react properly if you are firm and insistent. Some cats even learn to share living space with birds or other small pets. Once their curiosity about small creatures has been satisfied, cats will not only tolerate but also be a companion to almost any other animal.

Collars and Leashes

Nearly all cats accept wearing collars, but it is best to start them when they are still kittens. Some cats become so attached to their collars that they feel "undressed" without them and will not move until the collar is replaced if it has been removed for grooming or some other reason. You can fasten to the collar a plate or a tag with your name, address, and telephone number plus whatever other information you think might be important in case your cat strays.

Check from time to time to be sure the collar is neither too tight nor too loose. If you are worried that your cat may catch its collar on a limb or a nail and choke, buy the kind of collar that will expand so that your cat can squirm free. Some owners put bells on their cat's collar. Besides serving as a warning to birds, the bell makes it easy to hear where the cat is when you go looking for it in the dark. In some situations, of course, the bell might be a disadvantage to the cat, revealing its whereabouts to its pursuer. Some cats learn to use their bells as signals, shaking their heads to jingle the bell when they want to go in or out or when they want food or water. This is not something you teach the cat. Rather, the reverse is true, for the cat conditions you to respond to its bell. Even more amazing, some cats learn how to walk without ringing their bell. In this way they can be as stealthy as ever when they want to sneak up on a bird or some other prey.

Fewer cats like leashes, though some breeds, such as Abyssinians, take to the leash more readily than others. If you live in a city, using a leash may be the only safe way you have of getting your cat out on strolls. You should begin the conditioning early, **130** and never expect your cat to respond to restraint willingly. But if

you have your cat's welfare in mind, be persistent.

If your cat absolutely refuses a collar or perhaps accepts the collar but not the leash, try a harness. It may be more acceptable to your cat and is in many respects even more suitable for walking cats. You will never feel you might be choking your pet even when it struggles.

Climbing into Trouble

Cats are well equipped for climbing trees or poles—*up* but not *down*. If a cat would be satisfied with edging its way down backwards, it would have no problem, but a cat likes to see where it is going. Almost invariably it tries to come down head-first. It accomplishes the feat, too, but not with the grace that a cat normally displays. Unlike a squirrel—which stretches its hind feet straight out behind it, hooks in its claws, and then scoots down a tree almost as smoothly as it goes up—a cat puts its hind feet forward, trying to use them in the same way as when going up the tree. For some unexplainable reason, cats have never learned that in coming down a tree they have to brake themselves against the pull of gravity. However clumsily, cats do manage to get back onto the ground and seem well-enough satisfied with how they accomplished their descent to repeat the technique time after time.

131

With regularity, however, pet cats do get themselves onto or into chimneys, the wee outer branches of trees, the tops of poles, or in other predicaments from which they cannot escape without help. Their plaintive to frantic cries are confirming. Simple curiosity can be confoundingly troublesome. Unable to help their cat themselves, owners are likely to despair that their pet will ever set its four feet safely on the ground again. Rescue squads from fire departments or from the prevention of cruelty to animals organizations are schooled in how to handle such situations and generally get the embarrassed animals back onto level ground without mishap.

But why worry? If a cat does fall, it always lands on its feet—or so the story goes. This is essentially true. When a cat falls, it automatically twists its body—first the front and then the rear—so that it comes to earth feet first. With no obstructions in the way, cats have survived falls from four-story buildings without damage, but the shock of a fall from more dizzying heights could not be absorbed even by a cat's sinewy body. Very short falls that do not give the cat time to turn in mid-air can also be dangerous.

Yes, cats are good climbers, and they have a remarkable sense of balance that normally makes them masters of seemingly impossible situations. But like all animals, cats do make mistakes and have accidents; they are not infallible.

Tricks

Yes, cats can be taught tricks. The performing lions and tigers in circuses and similar shows are evidence of this. The common house cat is no less intelligent or responsive. The biggest difference is the trainer. Lions and tigers are trained by professionals who make their living by getting the big animals to perform. They know animal behavior well, and they take the time required to get the job done. If you go slowly and are persistent and persuasive, your cat can be taught to do many simple tricks. Keep in mind that a cat differs from a dog in basic psychology. A dog is naturally anxious to please its master and so is considerably more submissive than a cat, which is concerned mostly about its own well-being. It gets no personal pleasure from going out of its way to make you happy. You must make the reward for a good performance clearly the cat's. It is true also that some breeds are more easily trained than others and that some individuals can be trained and others not.

Basically a cat is taught to do tricks by bribery. They soon recognize that a satisfactory performance means a tasty morsel of food, something that they can get in no other way. Failure to perform results in a scolding. Repetition conditions the cat to respond to commands or cues. Make the training sessions short, but repeat them often. Teach only one trick at a time to avoid confusion. The repertoire can be expanded as each trick is learned. Shaking hands, playing dead, rolling over, sitting up, fetching objects—all of the common tricks learned by dogs can be mastered by cats.

Start the training early for best results. A four-month-old kitten is not too young to be started on a training program. An old cat may refuse, looking upon all the shenanigans as nonsense. **133**

Grooming

Cats are notably clean animals. Your cat spends a major portion of its waking hours grooming itself, going over every reachable part of its body with its brushlike tongue and using its paws to clean its face. The sharp projections on a cat's tongue are large enough in lions, tigers, and other big cats to shred the flesh from the bones of their prey. An affectionate lick from a pet lion can draw blood! The domestic cat uses its tongue to clean its coat and to put it back in order when it is ruffled. But even with all the attention it gives itself, a cat needs help from time to time.

Many cats look forward to their grooming sessions, especially if they were started as kittens. Be wise in your selection of times for grooming. If your kitten or cat is wide-awake and ready to romp or prowl, it will not be especially receptive to being groomed. Wait until it is relaxed and ready for a nap. Then the grooming will fit perfectly with its mood. Grooming is, of course, more essential with longhaired cats. To keep a long-haired cat in tiptop condition, it must be groomed every day.

You can get brushes and combs made especially for cats. Be selective and ask the pet-shop owner for advice. If you have a Rex, for example, you will want a brush with very soft bristles, because a Rex has no guard hairs. Similarly you will need longer bristles on the brush and longer, wider-spaced teeth on the comb for grooming a longhaired cat. You may also want a very fine-toothed comb for getting fleas out of the fur.

Be gentle if you find tangles or burs. First try to work them out **134** very carefully, a hair at a time. If this is not possible, snip them out with scissors. For a finishing touch, polish the coat. With the palms of your hands, rub the coat in the direction it normally lies, or you can use a chamois or a piece of nylon cloth. This not only makes the coat shine but stimulates the skin.

While you are grooming you can give your cat a thorough inspection. Check inside the ears and carefully swab them with a moistened ball of cotton. Ear infections are not uncommon in cats, but do not attempt treatment yourself. Consult your veterinarian. Look at the feet and between the toes for signs of infection or fungus growth. In summer, be prepared to remove an occasional tick if your cat is allowed outdoors. Regular inspections will keep its problems from becoming serious.

If your cat's claws are too long and sharp, and you have confidence in yourself, you can trim them. If you are a bit squeamish, have it done by your veterinarian. It is easiest if nail clipping has been part of the routine since kittenhood. Use only special nail clippers that you can buy in a pet shop. Do not use regular scissors. Clip only the tips of the claws, taking great care not to cut into the vein, a visible pinkish line. This is very painful and the bleeding is hard to stop. Do only two or three nails at a session. Let the others wait for the next time. (A cat has five claws on each forefoot and four on each hind foot.)

Only in exceptional cases, as with an uncontrollably destructive cat, should the nails be removed and then only the front claws. Without its claws, a cat cannot climb and protect itself. With claws on its hind feet, it will still be able to climb, though not as well, and it can fight back if attacked by slashing with its hind feet. Cats lose confidence and dignity from declawing, at least initially, but can adapt even to total declawing without traumatic effects.

▲ Lather the cat ▼ Dry with a towel or hairdryer

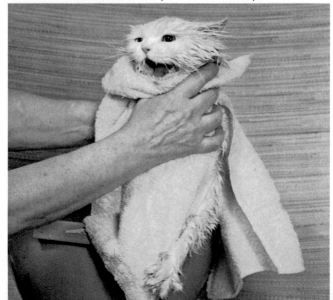

Bathing

Cats that enjoy being lathered with soap and soaked in water are indeed the exception, but some do. Others tolerate the ordeal and still others will not put up with it at all. But there are rare times when a cat must be bathed no matter how it feels about it.

Use only a very mild soap, not a detergent, or get a special cat shampoo at your pet store. If you have two laundry tubs, use them. Do the washing and sudsing in one and have the other filled with lukewarm water ready for the rinsing. Do not have the water deeper than your cat's armpits. Get the whole affair over just as quickly and as smoothly as possible, unless you have one of those exceptional cats that likes to dally. Then be sure to dry your cat very thoroughly, for cats catch cold easily. Never bathe kittens until they are at least six months old.

If your cat has a total aversion to water, you can use a dry bath to get rid of grease, stains, or odors. In some cases, talcum powder or cornstarch worked into the coat and then brushed out will do the job well. Dry cat shampoos can also be bought at pet stores.

137

▲ Brush the cat until completely dry

Traveling

What do you do with your cat when you go on vacation? If you are traveling in an automobile, you may be able to take your cat along. Most cats are not good travelers, however. They prefer staying at home and keeping to their customary routine. But if you do a lot of traveling you may want to start conditioning your cat to car trips while it is still a kitten.

First of all, get a good carrier—one large enough to accommodate your cat when it is fully grown. A well-built carrier will have vents on the ends and at the top, and it will also have secure latches and locks. This will keep your cat protected if you must leave it untended for a while. The top should be gabled, not flat. This will prevent anyone from stacking other boxes or bags on top.

Put your kitten or cat inside the carrier at home and let him get accustomed to it. Let him use the carrier as a place to take naps and to get occasional snacks. Carry him around the house now and then in the carrier. All of this is part of his conditioning. Then put the carrier in your car, and with the windows closed, open the carrier and let your cat do some exploring. In a day or so take the carrier to the car again, and this time take a short drive. Repeat this a number of times before you set off on a long trip. If the windows are closed, you can let your cat out of the carrier and allow him to ride on the seat or on someone's lap.

When you make stops on your trip and the door is opened, make certain first that your cat is either in the carrier or held securely by a leash. Cats can escape quickly, and in unfamiliar surroundings they become confused and will keep running until they find a place to hide. Then they may refuse to show themselves, not even responding to your voice. Most of the time,

keep your cat in its carrier at night, whether you are at a friend's house or at a hotel or motel.

Some motels and hotels will not accept guests with pets. Make your reservations in advance and make it clearly understood that you have a pet in a carrier. In those circumstances refusals will be rare.

While you are driving you will stop now and then for meals or to sightsee. Leave your cat in the carrier and also open the windows enough to let air circulate inside. Try to park your car in the shade and do not stay away long. A closed car becomes insufferably hot inside and pets can quickly perish.

Using the same carrier, your cat can be shipped by bus, train, or airplane, either traveling with you or taking the trip alone. Because airplanes are fast, smooth, and involve few or no layovers, they are the best choice if it is possible. If you are sending your cat by airplane, call ahead to make arrangements **139** and to make the wait at the air terminal as brief as possible. Check also with your veterinarian to get a health certificate that indicates your cat's good condition at the time of the trip's start. (If you are traveling abroad, be sure to check whether special entry or exit forms are required.) Label the carrier according to directions, and be sure you mark it as live cargo. Also buy insurance. All of these steps will make it clearly understood that your cat is valuable and will encourage reasonable treatment of it until the destination is reached. Line the inside of the carrier with shredded paper in lieu of the litter box, and if the trip will be a long one, fasten food and a water pan inside the carrier. A preflight soporific may be advisable to calm the cat's nerves; check your vet. Finally, make certain someone will meet the airplane at its destination so that your cat will not have to wait.

If your cat is not a traveler or you do not want to take it with you on trips, you may be able to get a friend or neighbor to take care of your pet while you are gone. It is best, of course, if your cat can stay at home and have someone stop by daily to feed it, change the litter, and do whatever else is necessary. Your cat will be lonesome, true, but it may be much more comfortable and safer than if it is traveling.

You can also take your cat to a boarding kennel. Ask your veterinarian to suggest a good one in your area. He may have accommodations himself, and while you are gone your cat can get an annual checkup. But check the boarding kennel carefully to make certain it is clean and not too crowded. Diseases spread easily in crowded conditions. If your cat is in good health when you leave, you should expect it to be in good health when you return. It will not be very happy, of course, until it is back home and in its regular routine.

Getting Old

A cat more than ten years of age is old, but many well-cared-for pets live until they are 15, 20, or even older. As age comes a cat sleeps more and moves more slowly. Infirmity is gradual and you must learn to be considerate. Your cat will no longer be able to see or hear as well, and so you cannot expect it to respond as rapidly as in days gone by. Keep your aging cat in a warm, comfortable bed. Older cats are more susceptible to colds and less able to recover. If it gets wet, towel it dry as soon as possible. Check with your veterinarian to learn any special attention it may require.

As a general rule, your cat's diet should be the same. Maintaining old routines is important. Some older cats prefer smaller amounts of food given with greater frequency, and they sometimes get more finicky than before, even refusing old favorite foods and insisting on new kinds. If your cat has been a good companion, now is the time to show your appreciation.

If regular cat food upsets your cat's stomach, try kitten food. Maybe the aged digestive system cannot cope with big pieces. Or perhaps there is a tooth problem. Let your veterinarian have a look. Some cats do lose their teeth and go through their last years gumming a diet of soft foods.

Remember the closeness of your cat over the years and tolerate your old friend in these waning days of his life. **141**

Your Cat's Good Health

Myth to the contrary, your cat has only one life and you are responsible for seeing that it is lived healthily and happily. Most cats, fortunately, are quite hardy. They can survive even in conditions no animal should be subjected to, but this is not to say they are comfortable. Many of these miserable waifs of alleys and abandoned buildings have known no other life. They do the best with what is available to them. Really less fortunate are the many cats that have been abandoned. They have known a better life, but have for some reason lost their comforts and human companionship—and they cry and complain about the loss, too. But your cat is lucky. It has a good place to sleep, regular meals, and somebody to complain to when things are not going its way.

Trouble is, cats are proud animals. They keep most of their miseries to themselves, and they cannot describe them to you, anyhow. You must be watchful and learn the subtle ways your cat uses to communicate its needs. You must also be ready to get professional help from a veterinarian.

Select a veterinarian early, as soon as you get your cat or kitten. He or she should be reasonably near where you live, preferably should have some sort of emergency service, and most certainly should like cats—which is something you and your cat can determine with the first visit. Your get-acquainted visit can be a trip to get your cat its needed vaccination to protect it from panleucopenia, or infectious enteritis. Two shots are necessary. One is given when a kitten is between one and a half and three months old, followed by the second or booster shot one to two weeks later. The veterinarian may suggest that addi-

tional booster shots be given at intervals during your cat's life. Depending on where you live and how freely your cat comes in contact with other animals, he or she will probably also suggest giving your cat a rabies shot. The manner in which the veterinarian talks and handles your cat will help you decide whether this is one you wish to turn to for help and advice with your cat.

First Aid for Cats

For most of your cat's medical needs you will not have to go to a veterinarian. In a special cabinet or box you should keep the basic items that you either use regularly or might need in a hurry if there is an emergency.

Flea powder or spray is one of the essentials, for it is difficult to imagine a cat going through life without getting fleas now and then. Your first-aid kit should also include such items as a rectal thermometer, petroleum jelly, a medicine dropper, mineral oil, cotton, bandages, and an antiseptic that is recommended by your veterinarian. Two or three tranquilizers —again, only those recommended by the veterinarian—could be useful, too, if your cat has an accident and needs calming. Then you can examine it or get it to a veterinarian.

▲ Checking the heartbeat

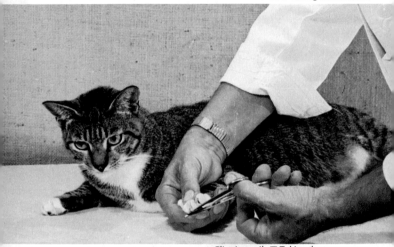

▲ Clipping nails ▼ Taking the temperature

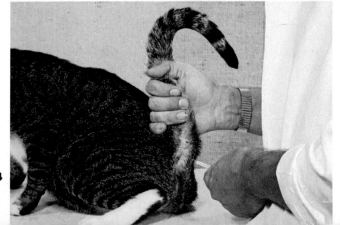

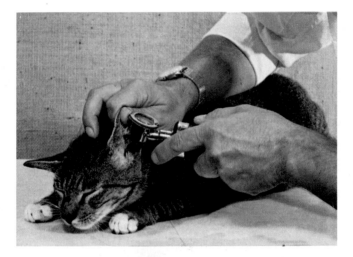

When to See the Doctor

You will know when your cat is not feeling its best. One symptom is a refusal to eat—that is, no interest at all in food as opposed to just being finicky. At the same time, the cat's normally bright eyes may become reddish or watery, its coat becomes dull and sheds more than usual, it vomits or coughs, and its breath becomes intolerable. Any of these is a sign of illness. Something as simple as an infestation of fleas could be the problem. Use the rectal thermometer to check your cat's temperature. It should be 101.6° F. (38.6° C.). If its temperature is significantly higher, take your cat to a veterinarian immediately. A high temperature indicates an internal problem that needs expert diagnosis and treatment.

145

▲ Inspecting the ears

Common External Ailments

Cats have fleas—their own special kind, in fact, just as dogs and humans do. But the three flea species—cat, dog, and human—will also infest the other hosts if they are sufficiently hungry and are unable to get the meal they prefer.

Fleas are external parasites that cause discomfort when they bite to get their meals of blood. Where fleas find good room and board they multiply and can in a short time become a plague. The bites are bothersome, of course, but they are only a prelude to more difficulties. Scratched areas are likely to become infected, and if the fleas are abundant enough the cat will also suffer from anemia, becoming susceptible to other diseases and infestations.

A variety of insect sprays and powders will kill fleas, but use only the kind that your veterinarian recommends. All insecticides are poisonous, obviously, or they would not kill the fleas. But since cats constantly clean themselves they can easily pick up quantities of the insecticide spread on coats. Your veterinarian may suggest using a powder and then bathing the cat soon afterward. Or he may recommend a repellent to be put on the comb or brush used in grooming the cat. Your job then will be to collect the fleas as they try to make their getaway. If you put the cat on a sheet you will be amazed at how many jump off. They can be picked up and dropped into a vial of alcohol to get rid of them. Some veterinarians suggest adding a B vitamin (thiamine) to a cat's food. This works as a systemic repellent to keep the fleas away.

Eliminating the fleas on your cat at the moment is just the start of the flea-eradication program. Adult fleas, which may live for as long as three years, lay their eggs on furniture, in rugs, or in

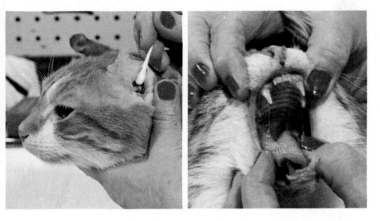

bedding. The eggs hatch in as short a time as two days or up to two weeks, depending on the temperature and humidity. The wormlike larvae that emerge from the eggs feed on dried blood or other kinds of organic debris found where they hatched. In about a week they enter a pupal or resting stage in which they transform into adults, emerging in ten days or two weeks. In getting rid of fleas it is quite possible to eliminate all the adults existing at the moment and still have a reinfestation from eggs, larvae, or pupae that remain.

All areas frequented by the cat must be thoroughly cleaned or vacuumed to get rid of these various stages. Even so, the defleaing of the cat should be repeated at least several times for a month or more to eliminate any fleas that may have escaped or just hatched. The pupae are especially resistant and may survive for several months in cool weather.

Worms

Several kinds of worms may infest cats, their presence generally signaled by such symptoms as listlessness, either a loss of appetite or a ravenous appetite, a dull coat, and either vomiting or diarrhea, sometimes both. Getting rid of worms requires a vermifuge, which is a medicine given either as a liquid or a pill that kills the worms or creates such an uncomfortable environment that they escape through the alimentary tract with the feces. Without exception, vermifuges are powerful. Remember that **147** they are strong enough to kill something alive inside something alive—your cat—and you certainly do not want to kill your cat.

If you think your cat has worms, get confirmation from your veterinarian. He will also be able to tell you what kind and can prescribe a vermifuge that is safe if administered as he directs. Avoid trying to get rid of the worms with a medicine you buy off the shelf unless you are absolutely sure of how to administer it. Worms are spread by eggs or other life stages that pass out of the cat's body in its feces. You must get rid of the feces to prevent reinfestations, and you must also give the cat clean bedding every day until you are sure the worms are destroyed.

Tapeworms of several species are common in cats. The eggs are picked up from the feces of other cats, from some kinds of foods, or from fleas. Larval fleas acquire the eggs, and as infected adults pass the tapeworm along when swallowed by a cat. One kind comes from infected mice or rats eaten by cats.

Roundworms are also common in cats, and a rather large population of these parasites can be supported by the cat without obvious symptoms. They live in the intestines, one species migrating as larvae through the lungs and liver before finally settling to an adult life in the alimentary tract. The eggs are passed from the cat's body with its feces, and a thorough sanitary program is part of the eradication process.

Hookworms also infest the intestines, where adults attach themselves to the lining and suck blood. A heavy infestation thus causes a general weakness and anemia. The eggs pass out of the body with the feces and soon hatch into larvae that regain entry either by being swallowed or by burrowing into the skin. Again, getting rid of the worms in the cat must be accompanied by complete sanitation of the cat's living quarters.

Skin Diseases

Sores on a cat's skin should be given attention as soon as possible, for the cat will lick the area, and depending on what it is, spread the infection. Get your veterinarian's advice. Some of the skin irritations loosely referred to as eczema are really difficult to correct if the condition is not taken care of early. Some may be caused by flea bites and can be remedied simply by getting rid of the fleas.

Mites, which are tiny animals closely related to spiders, are responsible for mange. The microscopic mites burrow into the skin, which becomes irritated and inflamed; the hair is lost in these areas and scabs form. Secondary infections may be worse than the mites themselves when the cat tries to relieve the itching by scratching and biting itself, opening the skin to bacterial invasion. If the mange is not treated, the mites simply spread, enlarging the areas of irritation and hair loss until death may result. Treatment involves use of a salve that kills the parasites, and to keep the cat from picking up the salve as it cleans itself, it may be necessary for it to wear an Elizabethan collar. This is a special hood, something like a funnel, that prevents the cat from getting its mouth to its body. Your veterinarian can tell you whether one is necessary and can either provide a collar or tell you how one can be made.

Another kind of mite infests only the ears, causing great discomfort. It can be recognized by a brownish discharge from the ears. You veterinarian will prescribe salves to sooth the irritation and heal opened areas, and he will also provide a miticide to get rid of the parasites. These mites are easily spread from cat to cat and their elimination is not easy unless a cat is isolated. **149**

Several other kinds of mites, even including chiggers, can be bothersome to cats. Whenever you see your cat biting or scratching itself, take a close look to find out why.

Ringworm, which is caused by a fungus, is still another common skin ailment. There are several kinds, but all are similar in how they affect the cat, causing intense itching as they grow and spread and resulting in raw areas and loss of hair. Secondary infections are common. Ringworm should be diagnosed by your veterinarian, who can examine hairs from the infected area under a special light to detect the fungus. Eliminating it is not easy, since infective stages of the fungus are easily harbored for long periods in the cat's bedding or wherever it frequents. This must be done, however, because the ringworm can also be picked up by humans.

Accidents

Cats have a curiosity that often gets them in trouble. Prowling under an automobile, for example, can result in a coat gummed with oil or grease. What the cat cannot clean off with its tongue will soil rugs, furniture, or whatever the cat contacts. Since some petroleum products are poisonous if taken internally in sufficient amounts, you must get rid of whatever your cat has rubbed or rolled in. Do this as quickly as possible by giving it a bath in a mild soap, rinsing and rewashing as many times as necessary. If you think the cat has taken in too much of what might be poisonous, call your veterinarian.

It is also unfortunately true that cats frequently come into conflict with cars. A cat is not a good judge of an automobile's speed, and cats hunting along a road at night may be startled and confused by lights and jump in the wrong direction. If your cat is

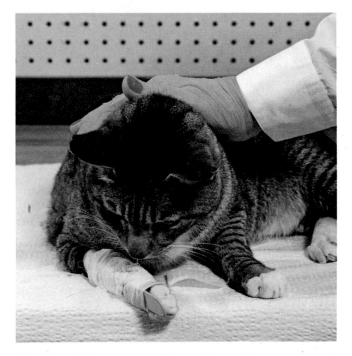

hit and is still alive, you must be careful in picking it up that you do not cause more damage. Lift it carefully, one hand under its shoulders and the other under its hips, and put it on a blanket or some other soft carrier. Keep it warm, because it probably will be suffering from shock, as well. Try not to change its position, so that in case bones are broken you will not complicate the fractures. If the cat is bleeding put handkerchiefs or cloths over the wound to help the blood to clot. If this does not work, apply a tourniquet between the wound and the heart. It can be tightened to stop the bleeding but must be loosened every ten minutes or so to prevent damage to other tissues that need the blood. Just as quickly as these preliminary first-aid measures are accomplished, get the cat to a veterinarian. No time should be wasted, even if there is no external evidence of damage. There may be internal bleeding, and you will need your veterinarian's skill to determine this and to treat the case. **151**

▲ Splint bandage

Internal Ailments

If you cannot see what's wrong but your cat is obviously not feeling well, you should by all means check with your veterinarian. Do not try to do the doctoring yourself, but be sure to follow the doctor's advice.

Hairballs commonly form in a cat's stomach, particularly in longhaired breeds, as a result of hair swallowed as the cat cleans itself. Regular grooming will help prevent this, of course, but it may happen anyhow, especially when the cat is shedding. Sometimes these balls of hair are passed out of the body naturally. Sometimes they are coughed up. If they become too large, however, they can be uncomfortable and constipating. Put a small amount of petroleum jelly in your cat's mouth, and hold the mouth shut until the cat swallows. This may provide the necessary lubrication to get the hairball moving. If this does not work you may need your veterinarian's help.

Panleucopenia, or feline infectious enteritus, is a very serious disease, sometimes incorrectly referred to as cat distemper. In kittens it is almost always fatal and most older cats also succumb if infected. Panleucopenia is caused by a virus that destroys white blood cells. The infected animal develops a high fever, loses its appetite, becomes listless, then goes into a coma, and dies. In the earlier stages it vomits a bilelike fluid. The disease affects cats differently but almost always violently. Treatment is possible but expensive and lengthy—if the disease is diagnosed quickly enough. Because of the commonness of the disease and its highly infectious character, vaccination of kittens is extremely important, with booster shots given annually.

Rabies does not occur as commonly in cats as it does in dogs, but when it does occur it is fatal. The chances of your cat getting rabies are very slim, but if you live where it can come in contact with other animals regularly, particularly wild animals, an immunization shot is certainly advisable. This is something for you to decide.

Flu is common in cats. The symptoms are similar to a common cold, but the viruses causing the flu are entirely different. Cat flu is highly infectious and may spread quickly where a number of cats are associated in a boarding area or even in a neighborhood. Treatment consists mainly of keeping the cat warm, dry, and comfortable, taking special care to avoid drafts. Pneumonia, a further complication, may develop if care is not taken, and to get your cat back to good health again will require medication and a great amount of nursing.

Infectious anemia is believed to be transmitted to cats from the bites of fleas, or possibly from the bites of other cats that have the disease, which is an acute anemia caused by a parasite that destroys red blood cells. Symptoms are listlessness, loss of appetite, fever, weakness—but these indicators may be quite evident on one day and then disappear the next. Without treatment about half of the cats that get infectious anemia die. Treatment consists of giving prescribed antibiotics, and in advanced cases, blood transfusions. Eliminating fleas is an important preventive measure.

Cats are bothered by several urinary problems. One of the more common of these is an inflammation of the bladder, or cystitis, which is evidenced when the cat has difficulty in urinating and may also walk with its back humped and its legs straddled. The danger is in the retention of urine in the body. It is essential that the cat be taken to a veterinarian immediately. Inflammations may be brought under control with antibiotics, **153** but if they have been caused by mineral deposits or "stones" that are still present and blocking the urinary track, surgery may be necessary.

Nephritis, or inflammation of the kidneys, is most common in older cats, especially males. Signs of the disease are gradual weight loss, thinning coat, excessive thirst, and increased urinary frequency. Treatment consists of trying to keep the cat as comfortable as possible to slow the course of the disease. With age also a factor death is the usual outcome.

Toxoplasmosis is caused by a parasitic one-celled animal that occurs commonly in cats and other warm-blooded animals. It can be acquired from eating raw meat in which the parasites are encysted, or it may be picked up from the ground where eggs have hatched out in feces. In heavy infestations a cat may have symptoms of a respiratory illness, or it may also become so weakened that it walks with a poorly coordinated gait. It also loses weight and is diarrhetic. Humans can be infected, but the body generally rejects the parasites before there is a debilitating build-up. Pregnant women must be especially cautious, however, as an infection may cause birth defects or even loss of the child.

Giving Your Cat its Medicine
Pills do not taste like fish or anything else that appeals to cats, and inside is the medicine, usually bitter. Not understanding the purpose of the pill, a cat is naturally reluctant to take it—and most generally quite stubbornly so. When a cat must be given a pill, you can only win by being more determined than the cat. Experience and know-how help. Your veterinarian can give a
154 pill with almost no trouble at all and will show you how.

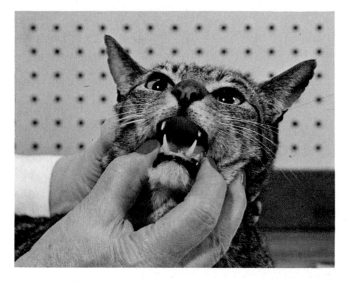

With one hand grasp your cat's head firmly, the palm of your hand on the top of its head. Using your thumb and fingers at each side of the mouth, force it open. Be as gentle as possible. If your cat struggles vigorously or you think it might, you may need somebody to help by holding its legs, both front and rear. To keep it from scratching, you may first wrap it in a big towel. After you have opened the mouth, lift the head up and tilt it back so that you can see inside. Put the pill on the cat's tongue and as far back as possible. If necessary, push it back with your finger. Now close the mouth and hold it shut. Stroke the throat to make the cat swallow. If your cat manages a deceptive gulp but still produces the unswallowed pill when you let go, repeat the process. This time coat the pill with a bit of mineral oil to make it slide more easily, or put a few drops of water on the tongue.

Giving liquid medicines is much the same. Put the medicine in a dropper, then open the cat's mouth and drop the liquid far back in the mouth. If the liquid is put directly into the throat, the cat may choke. Another procedure is to pull the lip away at the side to form a small pocket and put the liquid there. Don't be surprised if the cat spits a lot of it out. Do it again, if necessary, to get the correct dose, but never give more than prescribed. **155**

▲ Administering a pill

Cat Organizations

North America

American Cat Association
302B S. Brand Boulevard
Glendale, California 91204

American Cat Fanciers
Association
P.O. Box 203
Point Lookout, Missouri 65726

Canadian Cat Association
14 Nelson Street West, Suite 5
Brampton, Ontario
Canada

Cat Fanciers' Association, Inc.
P.O. Box 430
Red Bank, New Jersey 07701

Cat Fanciers' Federation
2013 Elizabeth Street
Schenectady, New York 12303

Crown Cat Fanciers Federation
1379 Tyler Park Drive
Louisville, Kentucky 40204

Independent Cat Federation
Box 1203
Southampton, New York 11968
and
31 Irving Street
Salem, Massachusetts 01970

National Cat Fanciers
Association, Inc.
1450 North Burkhart Road
Howell, Michigan 48843

United Cat Federation
6616 East Hereford Drive
Los Angeles, California 99022

England

Governing Council of the Cat
Fancy
28 Brendon Road
Watchet, Somerset

West Germany

Deutschen
Edelkatzenzuchter-Verbandes
6200 Wiesbaden
Rheinstrasse 49

International

*For information on cat organizations in
other countries contact:*

Fédération Internationale
Feline d'Europe (FIFE)
Mme. B. Kastengren-Remborg
Stenbrotsgatan 31
582 47 Linkoping
Sweden

Bibliography

For additional information on the care of cats and kittens, check with your veterinarian. There are many excellent pamphlets available free of charge.

Ames, Felicia. *The Cat You Care For.* New York: Signet Books, New American Library, 1968.

Bryant, Doris. *Doris Bryant's New Cat Book.* New York: Ives Washburn, 1969.

Carr, William H. *Basic Book of the Cat.* New York: Scribner's, 1970.

Dangerfield, Stanley, et al. *The Colorful World of Cats.* Connecticut: Longmeadow Press, 1975.

De Lys, Claudia and Rhudy, Frances. *Centuries of Cats.* Connecticut: Silvermine, 1971.

Eustace, May. *The World of Show Cats.* London: Pelham, 1970.

Fichter, George S. *Cats.* New York: Golden Press, 1973.

Gilbert, John. *Cats, Cats, Cats.* London: Hamlyn, 1968.

Grilhé, Gillette. *Cat and Man.* New York: Putnam, 1974.

Henderson, G. N. and Coffey, D. J., eds. *The International Encyclopedia of Cats.* New York: McGraw-Hill, 1973.

Ing, Catherine and Pond, Grace. *Champion Cats of the World.* New York: St. Martin's, 1972.

Johnson, Bruce. *American Cat-alogue.* New York: Avon, 1967.

McCoy, J. J. *Complete Book of Cat Health and Care.* New York: Putnam, 1968.

Mellen, Ida M. *A Practical Cat Book.* New York: Scribner's, 1950.

Méry, Fernand. *The Life, History and Magic of the Cat.* New York: Grosset and Dunlap, 1968.

Miller, Harry. *The Common Sense Book of Kitten and Cat Care.* New York: Bantam Books, 1968.

Pond, Grace, ed. *The Complete Cat Encyclopedia.* New York: Crown, 1972.

Pond, Grace. *The Observer's Book of Cats.* London: Frederick Warne, 1959.

Van Vechten, Carl. *Tiger in the House.* New York: Alfred A. Knopf, 1936.

Whitney, Leon F. *Complete Book of Cat Care.* New York: Doubleday, 1953.

Index

A

Abyssinian, 42–43, 130
Accidents, 150–151
African wildcat, 23
Aging, 141
Ailurophile, 37
Angora, 99–101

B

Balinese, 44–45
Bastet, 9, 10
Bathing, 136–137
Behavior, 126
Bells, 128–129
Bi-colored Persians or
    Longhairs, 41
Birman, 46–47
Black Death, 12
Black Persian or Longhair,
    48–49
Black Shorthair, 50
Blue-cream Persian or
    Longhair, 51
Blue-cream Shorthair,
    52–53
Blue Persian or Longhair,
    52–53
Boarding kennel, 140
Bobcat, 20, 22
Bornean red, 23
Breeding, 38, 41, 112, 113
Breeds. See individual
    listings
British Blue, 56
Bubonic Plague, 12
Burmese, 54, 55

C

Calico Persian or Longhair,
    94–95
Calico Shorthair, 96–97
Cameo Persian or Longhair,
    57
Caracal, 18, 20

Carnivora, 24
Carrier, 138, 140
Caterwaul, 32–33
Cat Fanciers' Association,
    Inc., 40
Catnip, 32
Cat organizations, 102–103,
    156
Cat shows, 102–109
Chartreux, 56
Cheetah, 18, 19, 20
Chestnut Brown, 63
Chiggars, 150
Chinchilla, 39, 58, 59, 89
Chinese desert cat, 23
Claws, 28, 29, 126–127,
    135. See also Declawing
Climbing, 131
Collarbone, 31
Collars and leashes,
    130–131
Color blindness, 27
Cream Persian or Longhair,
    60–61
Cream Shorthair, 60–61
Crystal Palace, 109
Cystitis, 153

D

Deafness, 28
Declawing, 28, 135
Domestication, 8, 10

E

Ears, 28, 29, 135, 149
Egyptian Mau, 62
Egyptians, 8, 10
Elizabethan collar, 149
Exhibiting a cat,
    102–109
Eyes, 26–27, 117

F

Falling, 132

Family of cats, 16–23
Felidae, 24
First aid, 143
Flat-headed cat, 23
Fleas, 143, 145, 146–147,
    153
Flu, 153
Food and feeding, 118, 119,
    121–123, 141

G

Gestation, 113
Governing Council of the
    Cat Fancy, 40
Greeks, 10
Grooming, 134–135

H

Hairballs, 152
Harness, 131
Havana, 63
Health, 142–143
Himalayan, 64–65
Hookworms, 148
Hunting, 128–129

I

Ice Ages, 16
Infectious anemia, 153
Infectious enteritus,
    152
Intelligence, 6
Isle of Man, 70

J

Jaguar, 20
Jaguarundi, 20
Japanese Bobtail, 66
Judging, 106–109
Jungle cat, 23

K

Kaffir cat, 23
Kennel, 140

Kittens: beds for, 124; birth, 115–116; children and, 36–37; choosing, 34–35; feeding, 121–123; newborn, 117; other pets and, 37
Korat, 67

L

Leashes and collars, 130–131
Leopard, 20
Leopard cat, 20, 21, 22
Lion, 19
Longhaired Colourpoint, 64–65
Lynx, 20

M

Madison Square Garden, 109
Maine Coon Cat, 68–69
Mange, 149
Manx, 70–71
Marbled cat, 23
Margay, 21
Medicine, administering, 155
Miacid, 16
Mites, 149–150

N

Nephritis, 154
Neutering, 111
Nictitating membrane, 26

O

Ocelot, 18, 20
Odd-eyed cats, 27

P

Palla's, 23
Pampa, 20
Panleucopenia, 152
Pedigree, 34, 103, 112
Personality, 6

Phoenicians, 10
Pills, 154–155
Pneumonia, 153
Pregnancy, 113, 114
Puma, 20
Purr, 32–33

Q

Queen, 112

R

Rabies, 152–153
Red Self, 74
Rex, 72–73
Ringworm, 150
Romans, 10, 12
Roundworms, 148
Rumpy, 70
Russian Blue, 75
Rusty-spotted cat, 23

S

Saber-toothed cats, 16
Scottish Fold, 76
Scratching post, 126, 127
Serval, 19, 20
Shaded Silver, 58, 59
Shampoo, 137–138
Siamese, 77–82
Silver Tabby Persian or Longhair, 87, 88
Silver Tabby Shorthair, 40, 93
Skin diseases, 149–150
Sleeping, 124
Smell, sense of, 32
Smoke Persian or Longhair, 84, 85
Somali, 43
Sounds, communicative, 32–33
Spaying, 111
Sphinx (Hairless) Cat, 86
''Sport'' breed, 41
Spotted leopard, 17

Standards for breeds, 40
Stumpy, 70

T

Tabby Persian or Longhair, 87–89
Tabby Shorthair, 90–93
Tapetum ludidum, 27
Tapeworms, 148
Teeth, 30, 31, 117
Temminck's, 23
Temperature, 144–145
Thiamine, 146
Third eyelid, 26
Tiger, 19
Toilet training, 126
Tongue, 31, 134
Tortoiseshell Persian or Longhair, 94–95
Tortoiseshell Shorthair, 96–97
Toxoplasmosis, 154
Toys, 127
Training, 133
Tranquilizers, 106, 140, 143
Traveling, 138–140
Tricks, 133
Turkish, 99–100

V

Vermifuge, 147–148
Veterinarian, 142
Vibrissae, 31
Vision. See Eyes
Visual purple, 27
Vitamin B, 146

W

Whiskers, 30, 31
White Persian or Longhair, 99–101
White Shorthair, 98
Witches, 12, 15
Worms, 147–148

Matt Warner is a professional zoologist who has made his living since 1950 as a writer and editor of books and articles on natural history. Above all animals, he has a special fondness for cats—large and small—and most particularly for the three that prowl his studio and paw through manuscripts with knowing inquisitiveness. This book was given careful inspection by the trio from start to finish.